TEACHER'S RESOURCE MASTERS
BLACKLINE MASTERS AND TEACHER'S MANUAL
GRADE 2

SPOTLIGHT on MUSIC

SERIES AUTHORS

Judy Bond	Michael Jothen
René Boyer	Chris Judah-Lauder
Margaret Campbelle-Holman	Carol King
Emily Crocker	Vincent P. Lawrence
Marilyn C. Davidson	Ellen McCullough-Brabson
Robert de Frece	Janet McMillion
Virginia Ebinger	Nancy L.T. Miller
Mary Goetze	Ivy Rawlins
Betsy M. Henderson	Susan Snyder
John Jacobson	Gilberto D. Soto

Kodály Contributing Consultant
Sr. Lorna Zemke

Mc Graw Hill **Macmillan McGraw-Hill**

INTRODUCTION

This *Teacher's Resource Masters* book contains supplementary activities for *Spotlight on Music.* These Resource Masters include the following:

- A variety of activities that reinforce or review concepts taught in the lessons. Some Resource Masters emphasize manipulative activities, while others offer opportunities for written or aural activities.

- Student and teacher support to complete the Creative Unit Projects. Students can use the Resource Masters to guide them through the project and complete a self-assessment at the project's conclusion. Teachers are also given an assessment rubric for each Creative Unit Project.

- Listening maps that provide visual guidance for students as they listen to specific music selections. The listening maps help students identify melodic and rhythmic patterns, tone color, form, and other musical elements. Suggestions for how to use these listening maps in the classroom are provided at the beginning of the Listening Map section.

- Review questions for each unit. The Unit Review Resource Masters allow students to record their responses to the review questions at the completion of each unit. The Read and Listen questions and music examples are recorded.

- Scripts and lyrics for the musical theater Broadway for Kids.

- Sign language versions of selected songs using American Sign Language.

All Resource Masters may be duplicated for classroom use. Each Resource Master is cross referenced to a specific unit and lesson that it was designed to support.

ACKNOWLEDGMENTS

Grateful acknowledgment is given to the following publishers. Every effort has been made to trace the ownership of all copyrighted material and to secure the necessary permissions to reprint these selections. In the case of some selections for which acknowledgment is not given, extensive research has failed to locate the copyright holders.

SEUSSICAL JUNIOR
Music by Stephen Flaherty
Lyrics by Lynn Ahrens
Book by Lynn Ahrens and Stephen Flaherty
Co-Conceived by Lynn Ahrens, Stephen Flaherty, and Eric Idle
Based on the works of DR. SEUSS

© 2001 by Warner Chappell Publishing Co., Inc., Hillsdale Music, Inc., Pen and Perseverance, Inc.
All rights reserved. Used by permission.
Copyright 2001 Ted Geisel Publishing.
All rights reserved. Used by permission.
Seussical Junior Libretto/Vocal book © 2004 by MTI Enterprises, Inc.
Broadway Junior and **The Broadway Junior Collection** are trademarks of MTI Enterprises, Inc.

Published by Macmillan/McGraw-Hill Education, a division of The McGraw-Hill Companies, Inc.,
Two Penn Plaza, New York, New York 10121

Printed in the United States of America
ISBN: 0-02-295851-7
2 3 4 5 6 7 8 9 021 06 05 04

TABLE OF CONTENTS

SPOTLIGHT ON MUSIC READING

SPOTLIGHT ON PERFORMANCE

SPOTLIGHT ON CELEBRATIONS

LISTENING MAPS

SPOTLIGHT ON SIGNING

Name _____ Date _____

School-to-Home Letter

Dear Family,

What an exciting, musical school year your second grader has in store!
This year your child will continue to learn new skills and concepts to form the
foundation for a lifetime of musical expression and enjoyment.

In our first unit your child will learn some basics about beat, rhythm, and
melody, including the pitches *mi* and *so*. We will also explore loud and soft
sounds and the tone colors of different instruments. You can help your child
discover these and other aspects of music in many ways, from attending
concerts or providing private lessons to singing, dancing, or listening to your
favorite music at home.

I am here to help *you* help your child find his or her place in a musical
world. Producing a music program at school requires a lot of work and
many extra hands. Thank you for whatever assistance you can offer this
year—be it at home, at school, or both. Together we can create a musical
learning experience for your child that will enrich his or her life for many years
to come.

Sincerely,

Second Grade Music Teacher

School-to-Home Letter

Estimada Familia:

¡Qué año tan emocionante le espera a su hijo de segundo grado en la escuela de música! Este año su hijo continuará adquiriendo nuevas habilidades y conceptos para formar los cimientos para una expresión y disfrute musical de por vida.

En nuestra primera unidad su hijo aprenderá aspectos básicos sobre compás, ritmo y melodía, incluso los tonos *mi* y *sol.* También exploraremos los sonidos fuertes y suaves y los colores de los tonos de los distintos instrumentos. Usted puede ayudar a que su hijo descubra estos y otros aspectos de la música de diversas maneras: yendo a conciertos o dándole clases privadas de canto, baile o escuchando su música favorita en casa.

Estoy aquí para ayudar a su hijo a encontrar su lugar en el mundo de la música. Hacer un programa de música en la escuela requiere mucho trabajo y muchas manos extra. Gracias por todo tipo de ayuda que puedan ofrecer este año, ya sea desde su hogar, la escuela o ambos lugares. Juntos podemos crear una experiencia de aprendizaje musical para su hijo o hija que enriquecerá su vida en los años venideros.

Atentamente,

Maestra de Música de Segundo Grado

Creative Unit Project

RESOURCE MASTER 1•2

Your project is to write and sing your own song! You will work with three other students. You will use the staffs below to notate the song. Follow the steps on the next page.

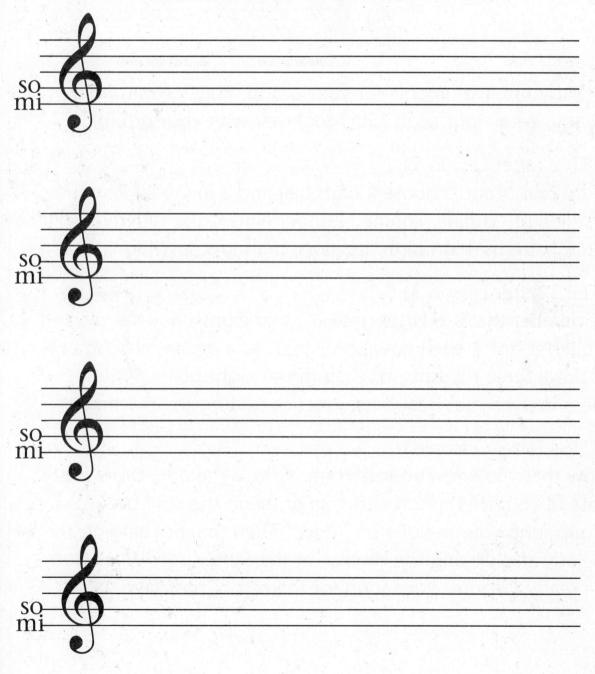

Name _____ Date _____

Creative Unit Project

STEP 1 (after Lesson 1)
Draw two equal beat bars under each staff for a total of eight beat bars, like this

Pick rhythm instruments for your group. Practice patting a steady, even eight beats. Stay together with your group!

STEP 2 (after Lesson 2)
With your group, choose a high bell and a low bell. Play the first line of "Engine, Engine Number Nine." Use different pitch patterns: high-high, low-low, high-low, low-high.

STEP 3 (after Lesson 3)
Remember that a quarter note ♩, two eighth notes ♫, and a quarter rest 𝄽 each equal one beat. As a group, choose one of these three rhythms for each of the eight beats. Write them in over your beat bars. Practice patting the rhythm.

STEP 4 (after Lesson 4)
Now that you know your rhythm, write a melody. Draw every note of your rhythm on either *so* or *mi* on the staff. As a group, sing your melody on "doo." Then practice singing the melody and playing the rhythm at the same time. When you are ready, perform your song for the rest of the class.

USE WITH GRADE 2, UNIT 1

Name _____ Date _____

Finding the Beat

Make your own shaker!

Step 1	**Step 2**	**Step 3**
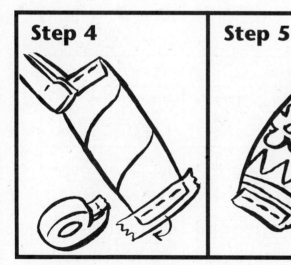		Popcorn Rice Beans Macaroni Fill to here →
Take a cardboard tube.	Pinch one end. Staple that end.	Fill tube halfway with dried beans, rice, or macaroni.

Step 4	**Step 5**	**Step 6**

Pinch and staple the open end. Tape both ends.	Decorate!	Shake a steady beat to the music!

High and Low

Make your own train pattern! Cut out the train cars and engines. Paste some cars high and some cars low in the boxes below. "Toot" your tune!

high			
low			

high			
low			

high			
low			

Rhythm for a Poem

Pick a rhythm to match the word below each beat bar. Choose a rest for each blank. Write the rhythm above each beat bar. Tap out the rhythm with a friend. Say the poem together in rhythm.

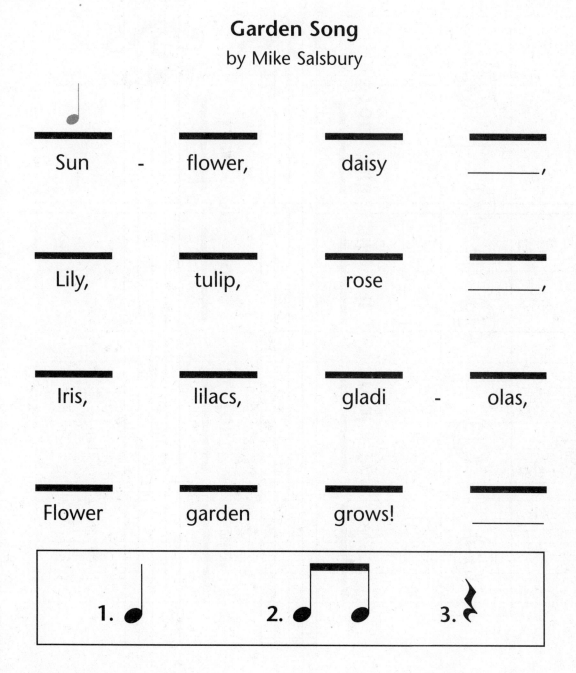

Garden Song
by Mike Salsbury

Sun - flower,   daisy   _____,

Lily,   tulip,   rose   _____,

Iris,   lilacs,   gladi - olas,

Flower   garden   grows!   _____

1.   2.   3.

Compose a Cheer

Make up a cheer to sell lemonade. Cut and paste the lemon slices like notes on the *mi* and *so* lines of the staff. Chant your cheer for a friend.

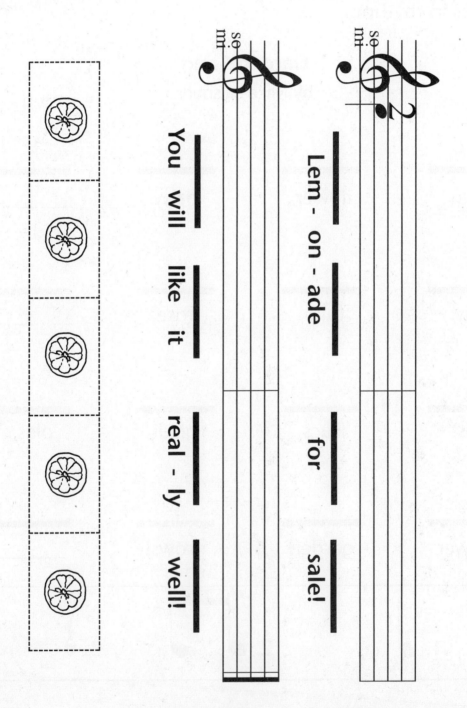

Name _____ Date _____

Mid-Unit Review

Draw a line from the word to what it means.

1. beat

a. the symbols used for pitches

2. melody

b. long and short sounds

3. notes

c. how high or low a sound is

4. pitch

d. steady pulse

5. rhythm

e. group of pitches

Draw a line from the word to its picture.

6. staff

f.

7. quarter note

g.

8. eighth notes

h.

9. treble clef

i.

10. quarter rest

j.

Rhythm Instruments RESOURCE MASTER 1•9

Woods

Metals

Shakers
and Rattles

Drums

Rhythm Instruments

RESOURCE MASTER   1•9

Paste the rhythm instruments into their proper families.

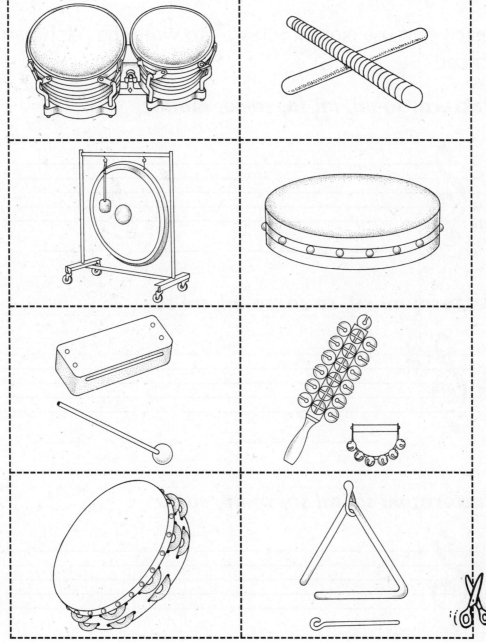

So and *Mi* Change Places

Practice writing pairs of eighth notes.

▬▬ ▬▬ ▬▬ ▬▬ ▬▬ ▬▬ ▬▬ ▬▬

On each staff use eighth notes ♫ to write the pitch pattern described.

1. Pattern: *so-mi, mi-so, so-so, mi-mi*

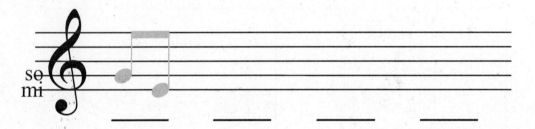

___ ___ ___ ___ ___ ___ ___ ___

2. Pattern: *mi-mi, so-so, so-mi, mi-so*

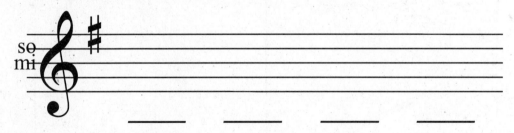

___ ___ ___ ___ ___ ___ ___ ___

3. Pattern: *mi-so, mi-so, so-mi, so-so*

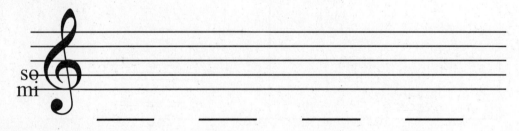

___ ___ ___ ___ ___ ___ ___ ___

Spotlight Your Success!

Review
Circle the correct answer.

1. Which word means how high or low a sound is?
   a. beat   b. pitch

2. Which word means the short and long sounds in a song?
   a. rhythm   b. beat

3. Which is the hand sign for *so?*
   a.   b.

Read and Listen
Circle the correct answer.

1. **Read** these rhythms. Then **listen**. Which rhythm do you hear?

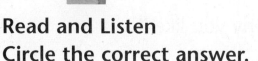

2. **Move** to show when each melody goes up and down. Then **listen**. Which melody do you hear?

Spotlight Your Success!

Think! Write or tell your answers.

1. How are beat and rhythm different?

2. Which instrument plays higher pitches? How do you know?

3. **Sing** "I'm Gonna Sing" and move your hands higher and lower to show the melody. How do the hand movements help you know where the pitches are?

4. **Write** about a song you like. Tell why you like it.

Create and Perform

1. **Create** your own melody using *so* and *mi*.

2. Clap this rhythm.

3. Choose one pitch for each note. Do not choose pitches for the rest. **Write** your melody.

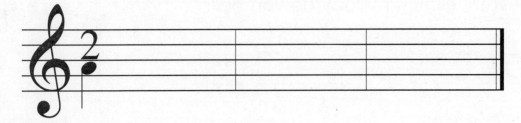

4. Sing your melody.

Name _____ Date _____

Self-Assessment

Who worked with you on the unit project?
Write everyone's name.

_____   _____

_____   _____

What did you like best about the project? _____

_____

What did you like least? _____

_____

If you could do the project again, what would you change?

_____

How did your group do during the performance?
The goals for the project are listed below.
Put an X in the box that shows how you did.

Goal	😁	🙂	😐	☹️
Our group was on pitch.				
Our group played the correct rhythm.				
Our group stayed together.				

Name _____ Date _____

Teacher Assessment

RESOURCE MASTER **1•13**

	Pitch	Rhythm	Stayed Together (Group)
Excellent	Sang securely on pitch throughout the performance.	Consistently played the correct rhythm.	Sang with sensitivity to staying together as a group.
*Competent	Sang on pitch for almost all of the performance.	Played the correct rhythm almost all of the time.	Stayed together as a group almost all of the time.
Progressing	Sang on pitch most of the time, but with some noticeable inaccurate pitches.	Played the rhythm correctly most of the time, but had occasional lapses.	Stayed together as a group most of the time, but had some difficulty.
Showing Little Progress	Sang on pitch some of the time, but had difficulty staying on pitch.	Played the rhythm correctly some of the time.	Demonstrated a great deal of difficulty staying together as a group.

Not Scorable: Did not participate.

*Competent is the expected level for all students.

Name _____ Date _____

School-to-Home Letter

Dear Family,

Do you enjoy clapping when you sing or listen to music with your child? If you do, that's great! In this unit your child will learn about the beats in music and how beats are grouped together in sets of two or three, with one strong beat per set. Think "OOM, pa, OOM, pa" (two beats), or "OOM, pa, pa, OOM, pa, pa" (three beats).

Clapping, tapping, stomping, or swaying to the beat can help your child master this concept. Make a louder sound or a bigger movement with the strong beat of each set. The beats in songs such as "Clementine" and "Take Me Out to the Ball Game" are in sets of three. The beats in many other songs are in sets of two.

Your child will also learn about the notes *mi, so,* and *la.* As you sing with your child or listen to music, notice how the melody goes up and down. Bring attention to how the notes move in the scale by moving your hand up or down.

In this unit your child will learn about the tone color of different instruments. How is the sound of a violin different from that of a flute, for example, or a trumpet? When you listen to music with your child, ask him or her to describe the tone color of the instruments to you. Can your child guess what instruments are playing?

Toward the end of this unit, your child will learn about A B and A B A forms. With the A B form, two parts of a song alternate, for example, a verse (A) and a chorus (B). With the A B A form, the opening part of the music is repeated after the B section. As you listen or sing, try clapping along with the first part of the song (A), stamping to the second part (B), and then clapping when the first part (A) comes around again.

The time you spend listening to music or singing with your child is time well spent. Don't forget to have fun!

Musically yours,

Second Grade Music Teacher

School-to-Home Letter

Estimada Familia:

¿Disfruta usted cuando hace palmas o tamborilea, cuando canta o escucha música con su niño? Si es así, ¡fantástico! En esta unidad su niño aprenderá sobre estos compases de la música y cómo los compases pueden agruparse de a dos o de a tres, con un compás fuerte por grupo. Piense "UM, pa, UM, pa" (dos compases), o "UM, pa, pa, UM, pa, pa" (tres compases).

Hacer palmas, tamborilear, chasquear los dedos, pisar o balancearse siguiendo el compás puede ayudar a su hijo a dominar este concepto. Produzca un sonido más fuerte o un movimiento más grande con el compás fuerte de cada agrupación. Los compases en canciones como "Clementine" y "Take Me Out to the Ball Game" se encuentran en agrupaciones de tres. En muchas otras canciones los compases están en agrupaciones de dos.

Su hijo también aprenderá sobre las notas *mi, sol,* y *la.* Al cantar con su hijo o escuchar la música, fíjese cómo la melodía sube y baja. Muéstrele el modo en que las notas se mueven dentro de la escala moviendo su mano hacia arriba y hacia abajo.

En esta unidad su hijo aprenderá sobre el color del tono de los diferentes instrumentos. ¿En qué se diferencia el sonido de un violín del sonido de una flauta, por ejemplo, o de una trompeta? Cuando escuche música con su hijo, pídale que le describa el color del tono de los instrumentos. ¿Puede adivinar su hijo qué instrumentos se están tocando?

Hacia el final de esta unidad, su hijo aprenderá sobre los esquemas A B y A B A. Con el esquema A B, se alternan dos partes de una canción, por ejemplo, un verso (A) y un coro (B). Con el esquema A B A, la apertura de la música se repite luego de la sección B. Al escuchar o cantar, trate de aplaudir junto con la primera parte de la canción (A), taconeando al ritmo de la segunda parte (B), y luego aplaudiendo cuando llega otra vez la parte (A).

El tiempo que usted pasa escuchando música o cantando con su hijo o hija es tiempo bien invertido. ¡No olvide divertirse!

Atentamente,

Maestra de Música de Segundo Grado

Creative Unit Project

In this unit, your project is to create and perform a ball-bouncing game song. You will work with three other students. Follow the steps below.

STEP 1 (after Lesson 1)

• Practice drawing half notes.

• As a group, make up an eight-beat rhythm pattern. Use ♩, ♫, ♩, and ♩ Use at least one half note. Remember that a half note is two beats. When you like your pattern, write it here. The beat bar after any half note should be blank.

• Play your eight-beat rhythm pattern.

STEP 2 (after Lesson 2)
• Make up a melody for your rhythm pattern. Here are the pitches to use.

do   mi   so   la

• Draw every note of your rhythm on *mi, so,* or *la.* Use the staff on the next page.

Creative Unit Project

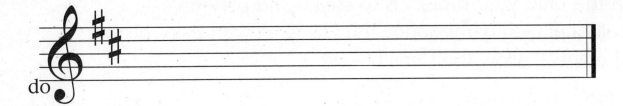

do

STEP 3 (after Lesson 3)

Practice singing and playing the song. Take turns. The others should pat the strong beat. Work on staying together as a group.

STEP 4 (after Lesson 4)

• Write your final song below. Add words if you like. Practice singing it. Clap on the strong beats. Stay together.

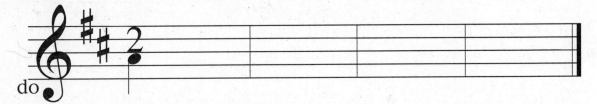

do

• Sit in a circle, and sing your song. Bounce a ball around the circle on the strong beats.

Sets of Two

RESOURCE MASTER **2•4**

Arrange the beats in sets of two for the meter signature $\frac{2}{4}$
Alternate strong beats and weak beats.

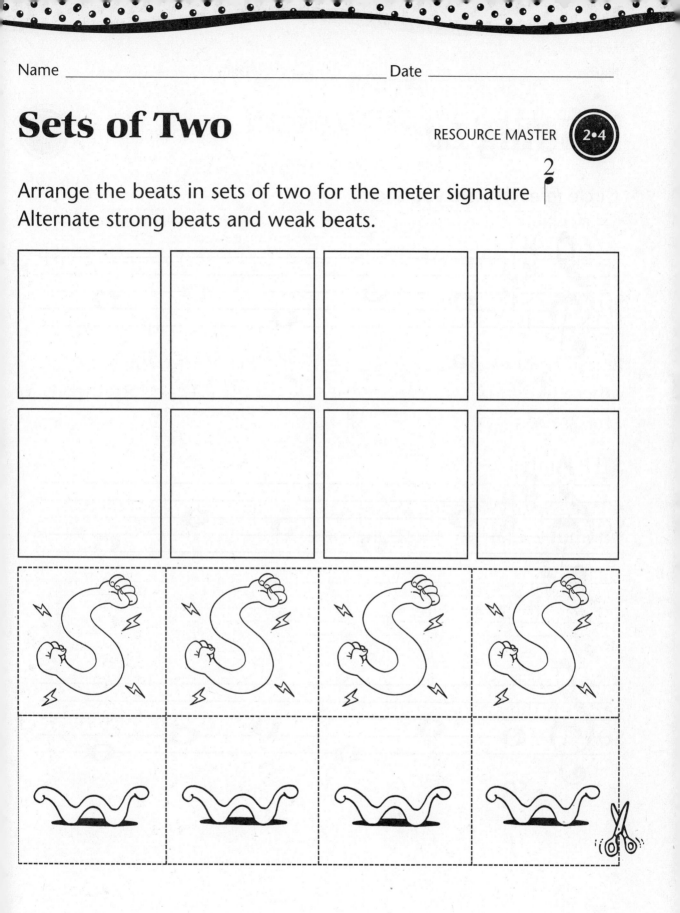

Finding *La*

Circle *la* each time you see it.

So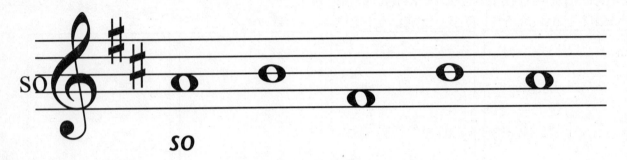

so

So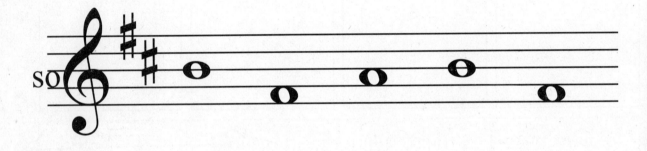

So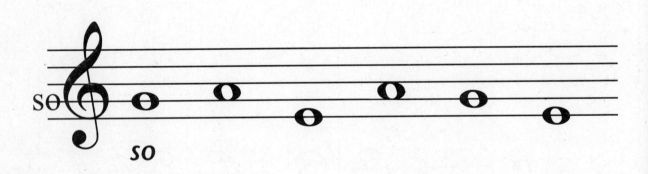

so

Name _____ Date _____

Circle the Strong Beat

Read this poem out loud. Circle two strong beats in every line.

Mary had a little lamb,

Its fleece was white as snow,

And everywhere that Mary went,

The lamb was sure to go.

It followed her to school one day,

Which was against the rule:

It made the children laugh and play

To see a lamb at school.

Mi, So, and La

1. Write *mi* and *la* underneath the matching note.

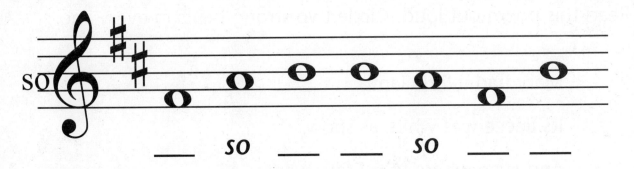

2. Draw each note on the staff above its name.

3. Write your own melody using *mi, so,* and *la.* Write the note names below.

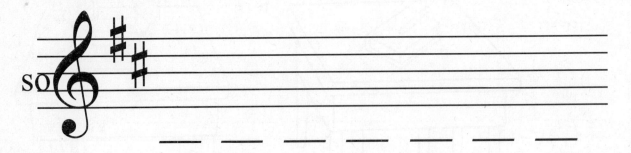

Mid-Unit Review

1. $\frac{2}{4}$ is the meter signature for beats in sets of two. Write the meter signature for beats in sets of three. _____

2. Draw a pattern of strong and weak beats in groups of three on the line below. Use a big *S* for a strong beat and a small *w* for a weak beat.

_____

3. Look at *mi* and *so*. Draw *la* on the staff above its name.

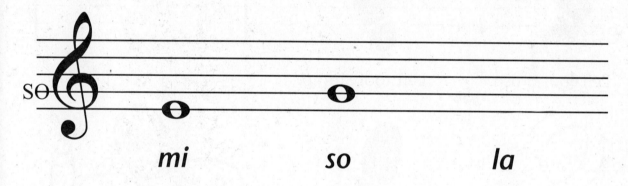

4. Draw in the notes on the staff above their names, and write in the names in the spaces below the notes.

Clog Dance

Here's a clog dance to do in section B of the music. Follow the diagram to learn how to do this fun dance!

Right foot brush,

Right foot stomp.

KEY:
Brush
(brush toe
forward
and back)

Stomp
(step firmly)

Left foot stomp,

Right foot stomp.

Left foot brush,

Left foot stomp.

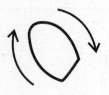

Right foot stomp,

Left foot stomp.

Repeat the pattern!

The Brass Parade

Color each brass instrument to match how you think the instrument sounds. Draw a line from the instrument to its correct name.

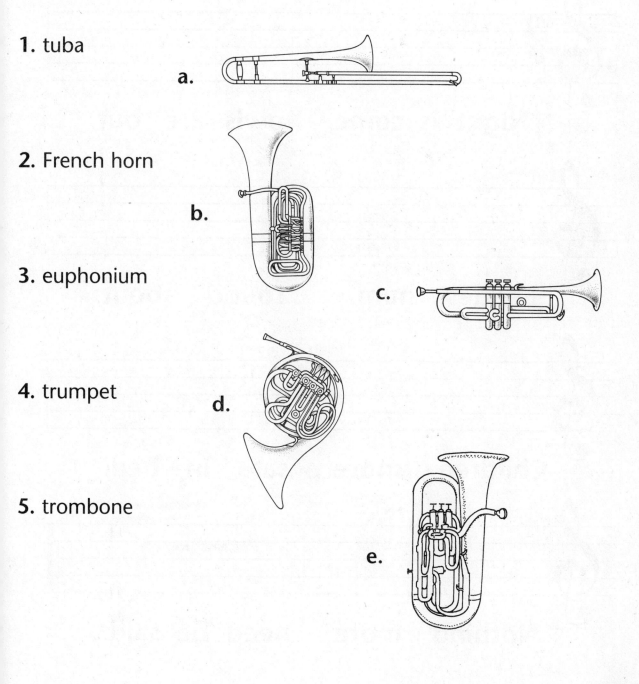

1. tuba

a.

2. French horn

b.

3. euphonium

c.

4. trumpet

d.

5. trombone

e.

Name _____ Date _____

Music for a Poem

Write your own melody for the poem "Finis" on the staff above the words. Use *mi, so,* and *la.*

Spotlight Your Success!

Review
Circle the correct answer.

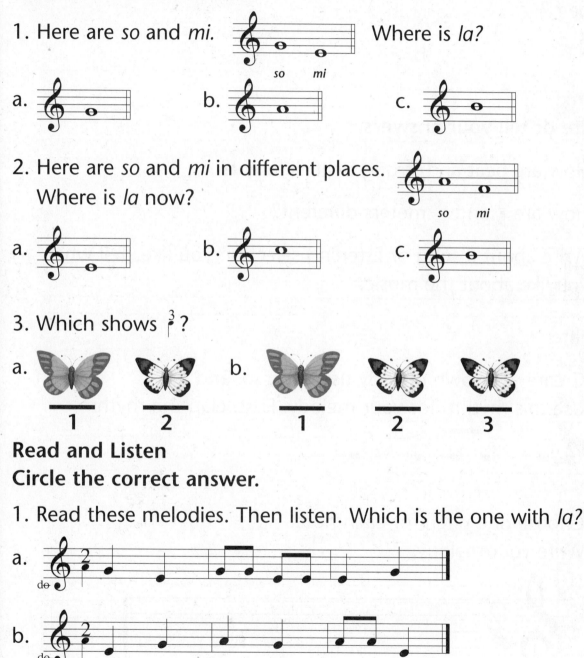

1. Here are *so* and *mi*.   Where is *la?*

   so mi

a.   b.   c.

2. Here are *so* and *mi* in different places. Where is *la* now?

  so mi

a.   b.   c.

3. Which shows ♩♩♩?

a.   b.

  1   2   1   2   3

Read and Listen
Circle the correct answer.

1. Read these melodies. Then listen. Which is the one with *la?*

a.

b.

Spotlight Your Success!

RESOURCE MASTER 2•12

2. Listen to the melody, and pat the strong beat. Is it in $\frac{2}{4}$ or $\frac{3}{4}$?

a. $\frac{2}{4}$ b. $\frac{3}{4}$

Think!
Write or tell your answers.

1. How are beat and strong beat different?

2. How are $\frac{2}{4}$ and $\frac{3}{4}$ meters different?

3. Write about a song or listening selection you like. Tell what you like about the music.

Create

1. Create your own melody using *mi, so,* and *la.*
2. Use this rhythm for your melody. First, clap the rhythm.

3. Choose one pitch for each note.
4. Write your melody.

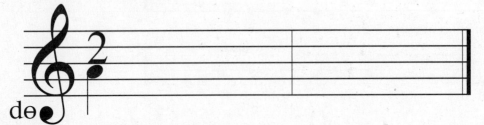

5. Sing your melody.

Name _____ Date _____

Self-Assessment

Who worked with you on the unit project?
Write everyone's name.

_____   _____

_____   _____

What did you like best about the project? _____

_____

What did you like least? _____

_____

Think about when you were writing your rhythm patterns
and melody, and when you performed. How did your group
do? The goals for the project are listed below.
Put an X in the box that shows how you did.

Goal	😁	🙂	😐	🙁
We could write our rhythm and melody.				
Our group was on pitch and played the correct rhythm.				
We listened and sounded good together.				

Name _____ Date _____

Teacher Assessment

	Notation	Pitch and Rhythm	Dynamics/balance
Excellent	Notated melody accurately with no mistakes.	Consistently played melody with correct pitches and rhythm.	Played in balance dynamically with the group all of the time.
*Competent	Notated melody with a few mistakes.	Played melody with correct pitches and rhythm almost all of the time.	Played in balance dynamically with the group almost all of the time.
Progressing	Notated melody with several mistakes.	Played melody with correct pitches and/or rhythm most of the time.	Played in balance dynamically with the group with some difficulty.
Showing Little Progress	Notated melody with many mistakes.	Played melody with correct pitches and/or rhythm some of the time.	Played in balance dynamically with the group with a great deal of difficulty.

Not Scorable: Did not participate (play) or did not notate.

*Competent is the expected level for all students.

School-to-Home Letter

Dear Family,

In Unit 3 your child will take a musical trip around the world, visiting every continent—even Antarctica! Each lesson presents something special about a continent: a song, a musician or composer, an instrument, or an animal.

You can help your child by asking which continent he or she is visiting and what interesting musical facts he or she has learned. What are some of the countries on each continent? Where is the continent on the map? Can your child sing you a song from that continent?

On their journey around the world, students will also be learning more about music notation, musical forms, and musical instruments. Students will learn how to recognize and draw half notes (♩) and half rests (▬), each of which has two beats. They will learn about the note *do* and where it is in relation to *mi* and *so*. They will learn the term *fanfare* and when fanfares are used. Can you think of a good time for a fanfare?

Your child will learn about gradually making music louder with crescendos and quieter with decrescendos. Ask your child to draw crescendo and decrescendo signs for you. You can try them out: as you sing a song, make a big crescendo and then a big decrescendo. How does it sound? How loud can you go? How soft?

This unit introduces the four members of the string family: violin, viola, cello, and double bass. Each of these instruments has four strings and is played with a bow. Of course, there are many other stringed instruments, like guitars and banjos, and more from other cultures and countries, but these are the four that your child will find in the orchestra. Ask your child to describe them to you. Which one is biggest? Which one is smallest? Which one sounds the best? Which looks easiest to carry?

Have fun with your child on his or her journey around the world of music.

Sincerely,

Second Grade Music Teacher

School-to-Home Letter

Estimada Familia:

En la Unidad 3 su hijo hará un viaje musical alrededor del mundo, visitando todos los continentes —¡incluso la Antártida! Cada lección presenta algo especial sobre un continente: una canción, un músico o compositor, un instrumento un animal.

Puede ayudar a su hijo preguntándole qué continente está visitando y qué hechos musicales de interés ha aprendido. ¿Cuáles son los países de cada continente? ¿En qué lugar del mapa está el continente? ¿Puede su hijo cantar una canción de ese continente?

En su viaje alrededor del mundo, los niños también aprenderán más sobre notas, formas e instrumentos musicales. Los alumnos aprenderán a reconocer y dibujar blancas (♩) y silencios de blancas (-), cada una de las cuales tienen dos tiempos. Aprenderán sobre la nota *do* y dónde está en relación con *mi* y *sol*. Aprenderán la palabra "*fanfarria*" y cuándo se usan las fanfarrias. ¿Se le ocurre una buena ocasión para una fanfarria?

Su hijo aprenderá a hacer la música mas fuerte al usar *crescendos* y más suave al usar *decrescendos*. Pida a su hijo que le dibuje los símbolos de *crescendo* y *decrescendo*. Usted puede probarlos: al cantar, haga un gran *crescendo* y luego un gran *decrescendo*. ¿Qué tal suena? ¿Qué tan alto, fuerte, llega usted? ¿Qué tan suave?

En esta unidad se presentan los cuatro miembros de la familia de las cuerdas: violín, viola, chelo y contrabajo. Cada uno de estos instrumentos tiene cuatro cuerdas y se toca con un arco. Por supuesto que existen otros instrumentos de cuerdas, como las guitarras y los banjos, y muchos provenientes de otras culturas y países, pero son estos los cuatro que su hijo encontrará en la orquesta. Pídale a su hijo que se los describa. ¿Cuál es el más grande? ¿Cuál es el más pequeño? ¿Cuál suena mejor? ¿Cuál parece más fácil de transportar?

Diviértase junto a su hijo o hija en su viaje alrededor del mundo de la música.

Atentamente,

Maestra de Música de Segundo Grado

Creative Unit Project

In this unit, your project is to write your own music! Your group will write a rhythm pattern. Then you will write a melody to go with it. Finally, you will perform your music.

STEP 1 (after Lesson 1)
Practice drawing half notes.

Create your own four-beat rhythm pattern. Use at least one half note. Write the pattern here.

Take turns playing your rhythm pattern. Use mallets.

STEP 2 (after Lesson 2)
Practice writing *do, mi,* and *so.*

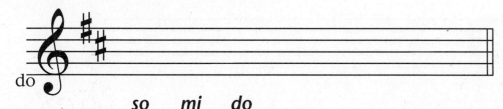

so   mi   do

Now write a melody using *do, mi,* and *so.* Match the rhythm pattern you created above.

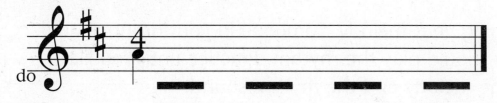

Creative Unit Project

STEP 3 (after Lesson 3)

Now create your own eight-beat rhythm pattern. Use at least one half note. Write your pattern here.

Take turns playing your rhythm pattern. Use mallets. Play the pattern with "Pata, Pata" or "Akinla."

STEP 4 (after Lesson 4)

Now write a melody using *do, mi,* and *so.* Match your eight-beat rhythm pattern.

Practice singing your melody. Someone in your group should sing. Others should play the rhythm. Practice until you like how both the melody and the rhythm sound.

Half Notes

1. Circle the half notes.

2. Circle the half notes, and then tap out the rhythm.

3. Write some half notes.

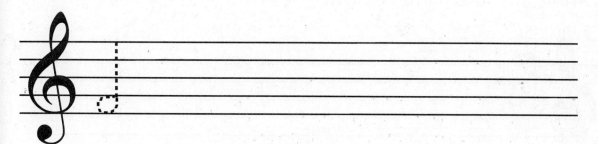

Do, Mi, and So

1. Write the name of each note below. Use *do, mi,* or *so.*

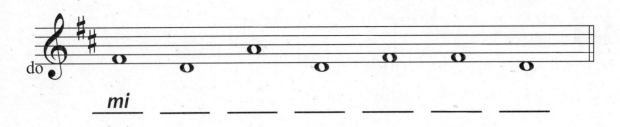

_mi_ ___ ___ ___ ___ ___ ___

2. Draw each note on the staff above its name.

so   *do*   *mi*   *do*   *so*   *so*

3. Use six notes and write your own melody using *do, mi,* and *so.* Write the note names below.

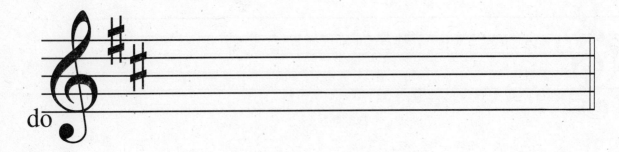

___ ___ ___ ___ ___ ___

Strings Make Music

The violin, the viola, the cello, and the double bass are four instruments in the String Family.

All four are made out of wood. They are hollow, with the same curvy shape and long neck. Each has four strings. The strings are tuned by turning pegs.

Each of the four is played with a bow—a long, thin stick with horsehair stretched from end to end. When you pull the bow across a string, it makes a sound. You can also pluck the strings with your fingers.

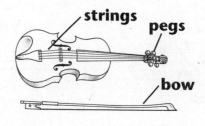

The violin is the smallest of the four. Next comes the viola, then the cello, and finally the double bass.

Fill in the blanks.

1. The violin, the viola, the cello, and the double bass have

_____ strings.

2. You play these instruments with a _____.

3. You can also pluck the strings with your _____.

4. The biggest string instrument is the _____.

Making a Duck Song

Cut out the six measures. Arrange them
on the music staff in any order you
choose to make your own duck song.
Then you can sing your song using
"quacks!"

Mid-Unit Review

Fill in the blanks with the correct word from the box.

A is for South _____, home of singer
Miriam Makeba.

B is for _____, the country of the Carnival.

C is for _____, a member of the String Family.

D is for _____, a pitch one step below *mi*.

E is for _____, a way of singing that helps us
know what a song means.

F is for _____, a short piece used to salute
or celebrate.

G is for _____, an instrument played in China.

H is for _____, a note lasting two beats.

fanfare	expressive	Africa	*do*
double bass	America	horn	band
half note	Europe	cello	globe
guzheng	Canada	Brazil	flag

Animals and Instruments

Animals in movies and cartoons often have special music that plays when they are on screen. On each blank line, write the name of an instrument to go with the Australian animal.

A **dingo** is an Australian wild dog. It has a bushy tail and sharp teeth. Dingoes live and hunt alone, in pairs, or in small family groups. They don't bark, but they howl!

_____

The **kangaroo** is a marsupial, which means that it raises its young in a pouch. A newborn is less than one inch long. It travels to the mother's pouch, where it stays for eight months.

_____

The **emu** is a large bird. It cannot fly, but it can run more than 30 miles an hour. It also can swim. The male emu sits on the eggs and looks after the chicks.

_____

The **bandicoot** is another marsupial. Its pouch is on its behind and opens to the back. Like the kangaroo, the bandicoot hops about on its rear legs. It sleeps during the day.

_____

The **brushtail possum** is also a marsupial. It has thick, warm fur. It nests in trees and eats leaves and grass. Its babies live in the mother's pouch for four to five months.

_____

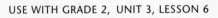

Name _____ Date _____

Crescendo and Decrescendo

1. Sing this melody without getting louder or softer.

2. Now sing the melody with a big *crescendo*.

3. Sing the melody again, this time with a *decrescendo*.

4. Draw a *crescendo* sign.

5. Draw a *decrescendo* sign.

Music Around the World RESOURCE MASTER 3•11

On the blank lines, write one musical fact that you have learned about each continent. It can be a song name, an instrument, or the name of a composer or musician.

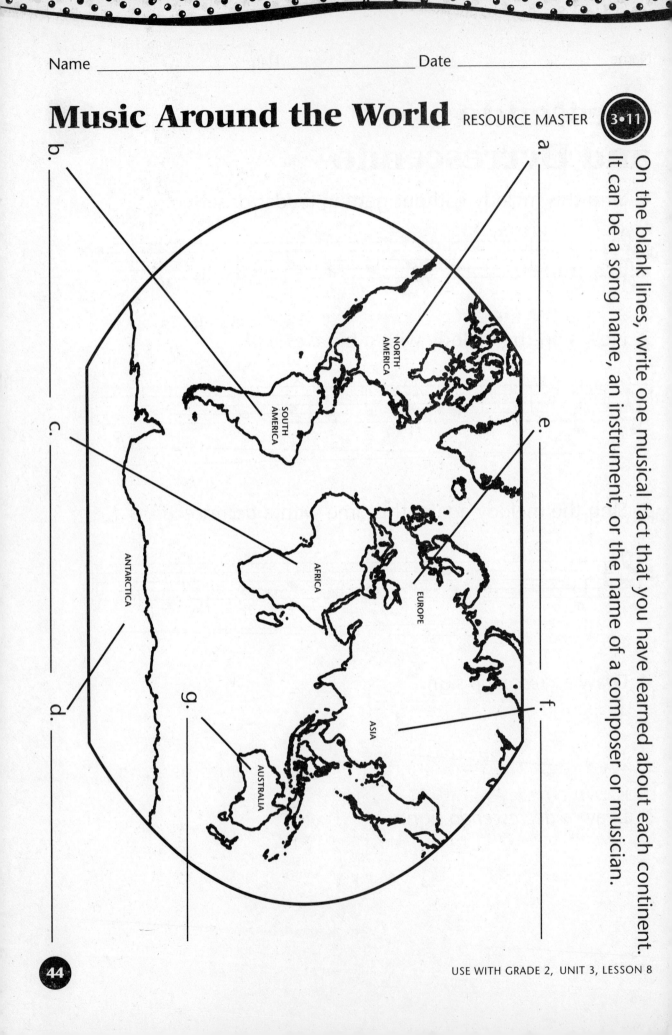

a.

b.

c.

d.

e.

f.

g.

NORTH AMERICA

SOUTH AMERICA

ANTARCTICA

AFRICA

EUROPE

ASIA

AUSTRALIA

Name _____ Date _____

Spotlight Your Success!

Review
Circle the correct answer.

1. Here are *so* and *mi*. Where is *do?*

a. around the third line   b. in the second space
c. around the line below the staff

2. Which instrument belongs to the brass family?

a.   b.

Read and Listen
Circle the correct answer.

1. **Read** these melodies. Then **listen.** Which uses *so mi do?*

2. **Read** these rhythms. Then **listen** and pat with the strong beat. Which do you hear?

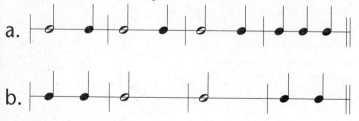

Spotlight Your Success!

Think! Write or tell your answers.

1. How is a half note different from a quarter note?

2. As you traveled in this unit, you learned about many instruments from different continents. Suppose you could learn to play any instrument from any country. Which instrument would you choose? Why?

3. **Write** about a song or listening you like. Tell what you like about the music.

Create and Perform

1. **Create** your own melody using *do, mi,* and *so.*

• **Clap** this rhythm.

• Choose one pitch for each note. Write your melody.

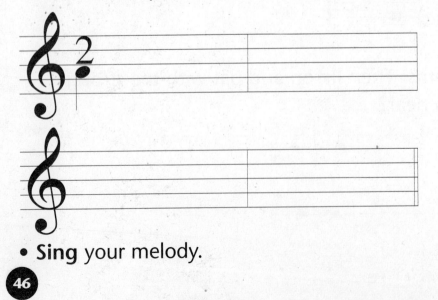

• **Sing** your melody.

Name _____ Date _____

Self-Assessment

Who worked with you on the unit project?
Write everyone's name.

_____   _____

_____   _____

What did you like best about the project? _____

_____

What did you like least? _____

_____

Think about when you were writing and practicing your rhythm patterns and melody and when you performed. How did your group do?
Put an X in the box that shows how you did.

Goal	😁	🙂	😐	🙁
We could write our rhythm and melody.				
Our group was on pitch.				
We used mallets the right way.				

Name _____ Date _____

Teacher Assessment

	Pitch	Mallet Technique	Notation
Excellent	Sang correct pitches throughout the performance.	Consistently used the correct mallet technique throughout the performance.	Notation was very readable.
*Competent	Sang correct pitches almost all of the performance.	Used the correct mallet technique almost all of the time.	Almost all of the notation was readable.
Progressing	Sang correct pitches most of the time, but with some noticeable inaccurate pitches.	Used the correct mallet technique most of the time, but had occasional lapses.	Notation was mostly readable, but with some unclear symbols.
Showing Little Progress	Sang correct pitches some of the time, but had difficulty staying on pitch.	Used the correct mallet technique some of the time.	Notation was difficult to read.

Not Scorable: Did not participate (sing/play) or did not notate.

*Competent is the expected level for all students.

Name _____ Date _____

School-to-Home Letter

Dear Family,

Have you ever heard the song "Do-Re-Mi" from *The Sound of Music*? This song names the pitch names, *do, re, mi, fa, so, la, ti,* and *do*. In this unit your child is continuing to learn these pitch names. The new one is *re. Re* is the second pitch of the scale.

Your child is also learning about music with beats grouped in sets of three and the time signature $\frac{3}{4}$ shown as in our book. Notes that are three beats long are written and are called dotted half notes. Help your child review by singing songs in $\frac{3}{4}$ time and clapping along to the beat. If you have music notation for any of the songs, look at the notes and rests as you sing.

Do you know any dances to music in $\frac{3}{4}$ time, such as a waltz? In this unit your child will learn about a dance in $\frac{3}{4}$ time from the 1700s called a minuet.

Your child will also be learning about musical phrases that act like questions and answers. A musical phrase that is unresolved (think of a five note scale going up) is balanced by a musical phrase that resolves (think of the same five notes going down again). You can play a musical question-and-answer game with your child, singing a few notes and then asking for a musical reply.

Music class introduces your child to a wide range of information about music history and culture. In this unit your child will learn about folk music and opera. He or she will be introduced to classical composers Frédéric Chopin and Wolfgang Amadeus Mozart and will learn about places in the world as diverse as Chiapas, Mexico and Wales.

Sincerely yours,

Second Grade Music Teacher

School-to-Home Letter

Estimada Familia:

¿Recuerda la canción "*Do-Re-Mi*" que menciona los nombres de los tonos, *do, re, mi, fa, sol, la, si, do?* En esta unidad su hijo continuará aprendiendo esos nombres de tonos. El nuevo es re. Re viene después de *do,* que es siempre el primero. Aunque su hijo no conoce todos los nombres de los tonos todavía, está perfecto que los cante bajo cualquier escala y que cante *Do-Re-Mi.* Cante los tonos hacia arriba y hacia abajo a medida que los menciona.

Su hijo también está aprendiendo sobre la música con compases agrupados de a tres y la armadura ♩. Las notas que tienen un valor de tres tiempos se escriben ♩· y se llaman medias notas punteadas. Ayude a su hijo a repasar cantando canciones en compás de $\frac{3}{4}$ y aplaudiendo al ritmo. Si tiene las notaciones musicales para cualquiera de las canciones, observe las notas y los descansos mientras canta.

¿Conoce usted bailes al compás musical de $\frac{3}{4}$, como por ejemplo el vals? En esta unidad su hijo aprenderá un baile en compás de $\frac{3}{4}$ de la época del mil setecientos llamado *minuet.*

Su hijo también aprenderá sobre las frases musicales que actúan como preguntas y respuestas. Una frase musical que no está resuelta (piense en una escala de cinco notas que sube) está contrarrestada por una frase musical resuelta (piense en las mismas cinco notas descendiendo nuevamente.) Usted puede jugar un juego musical de preguntas y respuestas con su hijo, cantando unas pocas notas y pidiendo una respuesta musical.

La clase de música introduce a su hijo en un amplio mundo de información sobre historia de la música y la cultura. En esta unidad su hijo aprenderá sobre la música *folk* y la ópera. Se le presentará a los compositores clásicos Frédéric Chopin y Wolfgang Amadeus Mozart y aprenderá sobre lugares del mundo tan distintos como Chiapas, México y Gales.

Atentamente,

Maestra de Música de Segundo Grado

Name _____ Date _____

Creative Unit Project

In this unit, your goal is to make up an improvisation based on the story "The North Wind and the Sun." Step 1 is to read the story.

The North Wind and the Sun were discussing which one of them was stronger.
The Wind argued on and on with much heat and bluster.
He said, "I am stronger by far than you. Can you not see how the trees bend before me?"
The Sun smiled and quietly answered, "Yes, they bend, but you are wrong."
The North Wind snapped, "No, it is clearly you who are wrong. I am right."
Just then, a Traveler passed along, wrapped in a long, black cloak.
The Sun said, "Let us agree on one thing."
"What is that?" said the North Wind.
"The one who can strip that traveler of his cloak is stronger."
The North Wind growled, "Very well. I agree. You shall soon see who is stronger!"
The Sun said politely, "Your turn first, North Wind!"
The North Wind nodded confidently.
He sent a cold, fierce blast of wind at the Traveler.
The North Wind boasted, "Look at how my icy gust whipped at the Traveler's cloak!"
The Sun answered, "Ah, yes, but do you notice that the Traveler is still wearing it?"
Indeed, the Traveler was wrapping the cloak even more tightly around his body!
The Sun said, "Better try again!"
The North Wind snarled, "Humph! There is nothing on this Earth that can resist me!"
He sent an even colder, even stronger blast of howling wind straight at the Traveler.
The wind was so overpowering that the Traveler could barely stand!
Nonetheless, the Traveler wrapped the coat still tighter around himself.
The North Wind was furious! He knew that there was nothing more that he could do!
The Sun smiled and said, "I believe it is now my turn, is it not? Here goes!"
The Sun began to shine. At first, his beams were gentle.
The warmth seemed pleasant to the Traveler after the bitter cold of the North Wind.
The Traveler unfastened the collar of his cloak.
The Sun's rays grew even warmer.
The Traveler smiled, opened his cloak and let it fall back loosely from his shoulders.
The Sun's rays grew truly hot!
The Traveler pulled off his cloak and mopped his brow.
To escape the blazing sunshine, he threw himself down in the shade of a roadside tree.
The Sun smiled.
He had won the contest!

Moral: Gentleness and kind persuasion win where force and bluster fail.

Creative Unit Project

RESOURCE MASTER 4•3

STEP 2 (after Lesson 2)
• Work with a partner. One of you should play the Sun, and the other the North Wind. Have a conversation as if you were the two characters.
• Now take turns improvising a "conversation" with notes instead of words. Use *do, re, mi,* and *so* in G (GAB D). One partner should play "questions," ending on *so.* The other partner should play "answers," ending on *do.*

STEP 3 (after Lesson 3)
• Discuss how you can use your musical question-and-answer patterns in your performance. Think about the sound of your notes. How can you use these ideas in your music to match the story meaning?
— *piano, forte*   — *fast, slow*
— *crescendo, decrescendo*

You might also try using C pentatonic (CDE GA) in your questions and answers. Begin on *do.* End questions on *so* and statements on *do.*
• Which instruments will you use for the different parts?
• How will you use movement in your performance?
• Will you have a narrator? How about sound effects?
Keep trying out your ideas until you like the results.

STEP 4
Stage your performance of "The North Wind and the Sun."
If you like, signal "The End" with two notes played on all instruments.

Name _____ Date _____

One, Two, or Three Beats

1. How many beats are in each note and rest? On the lines below, write 1, 2, or 3.

1 ___ ___ ___ ___ ___ ___ ___

2. Practice writing ♩ _____ ♩ _____ ♩ _____ ♩. _____.

3. Write your own rhythm pattern in ³₄ meter. Use notes or rests that match the number of beats shown under the beat bars.

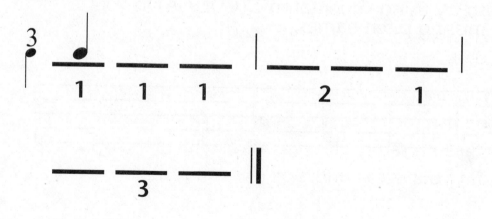

4. Tap out the rhythms in each line of music.

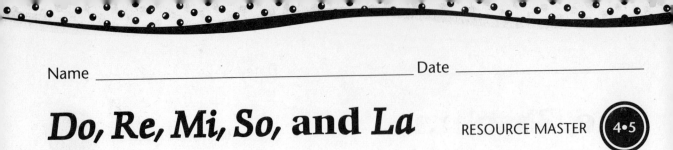

Name _____ Date _____

Do, Re, Mi, So, and La   RESOURCE MASTER 4•5

1. Look at the notes and pitch names below.

do   re   mi   so   la

2. Write ♩. to show the missing pitches.

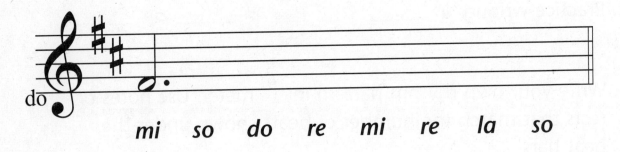

mi   so   do   re   mi   re   la   so

3. Fill in the missing pitch names.

___ ___ ___ ___ ___ ___

The Rhythm of the Wind

Cut out the notes and rests. Place them on the staffs to create rhythms that remind you of two types of wind. Play one of your patterns and have others guess what it is.

Slow Summer Wind

Fast Fall Wind

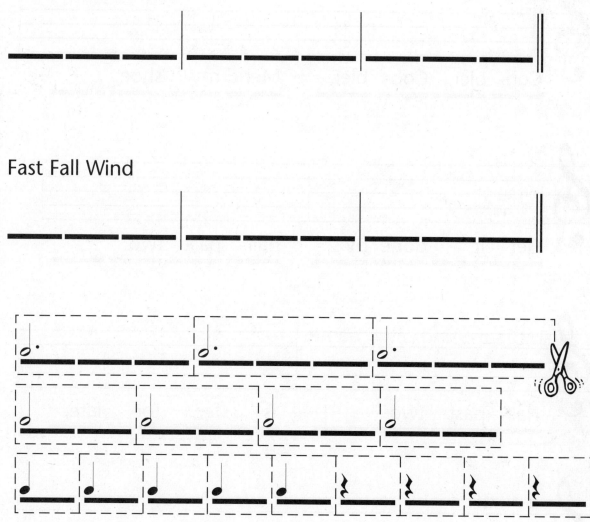

Composing with Pitches

Write your own melody for "Cobbler, Cobbler" on the staff above the words. Use *do, re, mi, so,* and *la.* Make sure that each measure has four beats. (Create your rhythm first!)

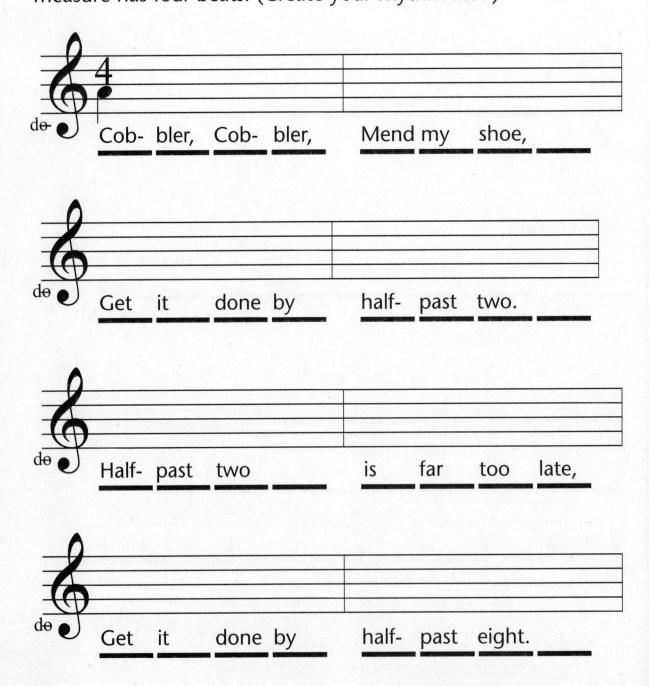

Mid-Unit Review

1. Add the missing quarter note, quarter rest, half note, or dotted half note to each measure so that it has exactly three beats.

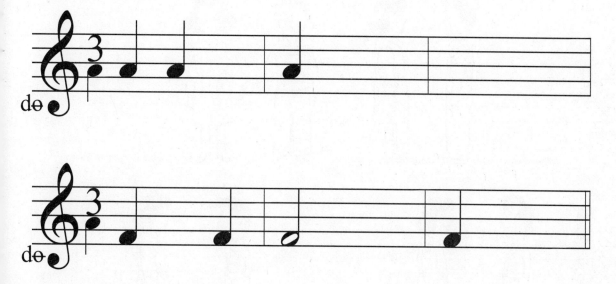

2. Circle *re* each time you see it. Fill in the blanks below with the missing pitch names.

___ ___ ___ ___ ___ ___ ___ ___ ___ ___

3. An *étude* is

    a. a piano.   **b.** a composer.   **c.** a music exercise.

Dancing a Minuet

Make up a minuet by putting together these moves in any order. To start, either face your partner or stand side to side.

 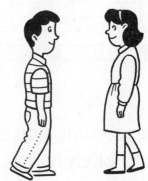

1. Step front (and back).   **2.** Step back (and back).

3. Step side (and back).   **4.** Bow or curtsy.

Musical Questions and Answers

 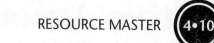

Sing or play each line of music. Write **Q** in the box if the line is a question phrase, and **A** if it is an answer phrase.

1.

2.

3.

4. Use quarter notes and create your own question or answer phrase using *do, re, mi,* and *so*. Write **Q** or **A** in the box.

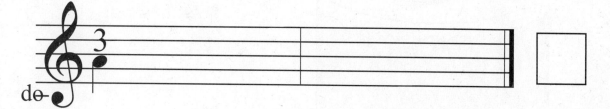

Native American Music

Native American music is used on many different occasions. There are different kinds of music for children, for games, for helping the sick, and to honor people who have done good things for their community. There are also many dances that go with Native American music. One type of Native American event that has a lot of music and dances is called a powwow. Native American people from all over the United States participate in powwows.

Three musical instruments often used in Native American music are the wooden flute, the drum, and the rattle. Which are the rhythm instruments? Color them blue.

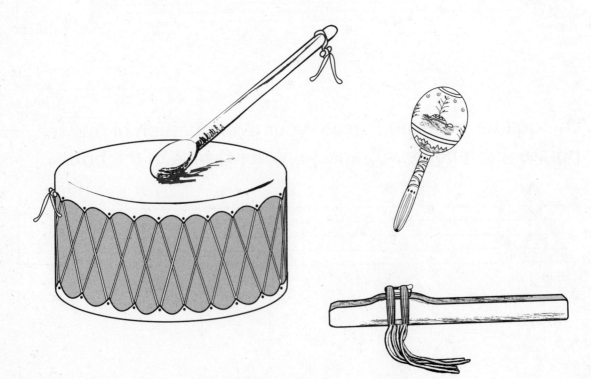

Name _____ Date _____

Spotlight Your Success!

Review
Circle the correct answer.

1. How many beats does a dotted half note last for in ¾ time?
   - a. 1
   - b. 2
   - c. 3
   - d. 4

2. Which is the hand sign for *re?*

   a.

   b.

Read and Listen
Read these patterns. Then listen. Which do you hear?
Circle the correct answer.

1. Which pattern has only *do, re,* and *mi?*

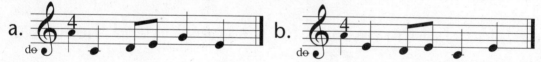

2. Which rhythm pattern has a dotted half note?

   a. 2/4 ♩ ♩ | ♩ ♩ | ♩ ♩ | 𝄂

   b. 3/4 𝅗𝅥. | ♩ ♩ ♩ | ♩ 𝅗𝅥 | 𝄂

Spotlight Your Success!

Think! Write or tell your answers.

1. Which of these songs are folk songs? Circle the titles.
   How do you know?

   Hello, Hello There   *Chiapanecas*   *Old Woman and the Pig*

2. **Write** about a song or listening you like. Tell why you like it.

Create

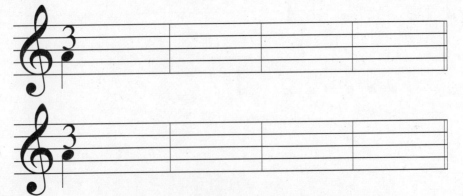

1. **Read** and clap the rhythms for the question and the answer
   with a partner.

2. **Create** a melody using *do, re, mi,* and *so* for each part. End the
   question on *so.* End the answer on *do.* Write your melodies.

Perform your question and answer, taking turns.

Name _____ Date _____

Self-Assessment

Who worked with you on the unit project?
Write everyone's name.

_____   _____

_____   _____

What did you like best about the project? _____

_____

What did you like least? _____

_____

Think about your performance. How did your group do?
Put an X in the box that shows how you did.

Goal	😁	🙂	😐	🙁
Our movements and sounds were interesting.				
Our performance matched the meaning of the story.				
We all took part in the performance.				

Name _____ Date _____

Teacher Assessment

	Musical or Dramatic Improvisation	Creative Choices	Group Participation
Excellent	Spontaneously created an innovative improvisation using movements and sound that resulted in an interesting, cohesive performance.	Creative choices enhanced the story.	All participated throughout the performance.
*Competent	Spontaneously created an improvisation using movements and sound that resulted in a cohesive performance.	Creative choices supported the story.	Most participated throughout the performance.
Progressing	Spontaneously created an improvisation using movements or sound that resulted in a performance.	Creative choices conveyed the story, but at times detracted from it.	Some participated throughout the performance.
Showing Little Progress	Spontaneously created an improvisation using movements or sound that resulted in a disjointed performance.	Creative choices detracted from the story.	Few participated throughout the performance.

Not Scorable: Did not participate.

*Competent is the expected level for all students.

School-to-Home Letter

Dear Family,

In music class Unit 5 begins with a song called "Everybody Has Music Inside." We will be working in school to bring out that music in each child. Over the next few weeks we will learn about the dotted quarter note ♩., the pentatonic scale, and *ritando* and *accelerando*. Ask your child how many eighth notes can fit in the length of a dotted quarter note (3), and how many pitches are in a pentatonic song (5). Practice singing a song by gradually speeding up (*accelerando*) and then gradually slowing down (*ritando*) at the end.

In this unit your child will also learn about a variety of musical styles, including a Latin American folk song, a sea chantey, and Dixieland. He or she will discover music and games from China, Germany, and Cyprus, as well as some American favorites. Students will play instruments with the Creole party music called *zydeco* and learn about Orff instruments from Africa, Indonesia, and Germany.

Ask your child what his or her favorite kind of music is from Unit 5. If possible, listen to this kind of music at home with your child. Clap to the beat, and make up a dance. Have fun!

Sincerely,

Second Grade Music Teacher

School-to-Home Letter

Estimada Familia:

La Unidad 5 de la clase de música comienza con una canción llamada "Everybody Has Music Inside" y trabajaremos en la escuela para que cada niño aprenda esa canción. Durante las siguientes semanas aprenderemos sobre la negra punteada ♩. la escala pentatónica y el retardo (ritando) y el accelerando. Pregunte a su hijo cuántas corcheas pueden entrar en la longitud de una negra punteada (3), y cuántos tonos hay en una canción pentatónica (5). Practique cantar una canción acelerando gradualmente (accelerando) y luego desacelerando gradualmente (ritando) al final.

En esta unidad su hijo también aprenderá sobre una variedad de estilos musicales, incluyendo el baile country, el 'sea chantey' y Dixieland. Él o ella descubrirán la música y los juegos de China, Alemania y Chipre, y algunos favoritos de los Estados Unidos. Los alumnos jugarán al ritmo de la música creole llamada Zydeco y aprenderán sobre los instrumentos Orff de África, Indonesia y Alemania.

Pregunte a su hijo cuál es su tipo favorito de música dentro de la Unidad 5. Si es posible, escuche ese tipo de música en casa con su hijo o hija. Hagan palmas siguiendo el ritmo e inventen una danza.

Atentamente,

Maestra de Música de Segundo Grado

Creative Unit Project

RESOURCE MASTER 5•2

For your project, you will set a funny poem about animals to music. You will write the rhythm and the melody. You will think about the feelings of the poem. Then you will perform your song.

STEP 1 (after Lesson 1)
Learn the poem. Say it aloud in rhythm.

"Higglety, Pigglety, Pop!" by Samuel Goodrich

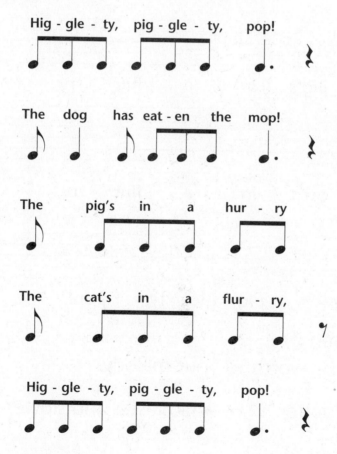

STEP 2 (after Lesson 2)
Now you can create a melody for the poem. Work in a small group. Here are the pitches to use.

do re mi so la

Creative Unit Project

do

Hig - gle - ty, pig - gle - ty, pop!

The dog has eat - en the mop!

The pig's in a hur - ry

The cat's in a flur - ry,

Hig - gle - ty, pig - gle - ty, pop!

STEP 3 (after Lesson 3)
Practice singing the words to your melody.

• Get louder and softer. • Go faster and slower.

STEP 4 (after Lesson 4)
Now work with the whole class to write a four-beat rhythm ostinato. You will use the ostinato when you perform. Be sure to practice all of the different parts. Then perform!

Find the Rhythm

Create a rhythm to go with the poem "The Elephant Carries a Great Big Trunk." Cut out the rhythm patterns. Paste them above the words they match best.

2.

1.

The   elephant carries a

2.

great big trunk.

3.

He   never packs it with

4.

clothes;

5.

It   has no lock, and it

6.

has no key;

7.

But he   takes it wherever he

8.

goes.

a.

b.

c.

d.

e.   f.   g.   h.

Pentatonic Scale

RESOURCE MASTER 5•5

Below are three songs that start with pitches from the pentatonic (five note) scale. Write notes on each staff to match the pitch names. Then try singing the pitches to guess the name of each song.

Have your teacher help you write the title in the space above the staff.

do | re | mi | so | la

Pentatonic Scale

1. _____

do   re   mi   mi   re   do   re   mi   do   so (low)

2. _____

(low) so   do   do   do   do   do   re   mi   mi   mi   mi   mi

3. _____

(low) do (high) do la so mi so re (low) do (high) do la so mi so

Name _____ Date _____

World Games

All around the world, people like to play musical games.

Two Tigers

This game from China is a little like Duck, Duck, Goose. To play, you will need one "tiger tail"—a piece of rope or yarn or a belt. All players sit in a circle. One player is given the tail and walks around the outside of the circle while the group sings this song. (You may use the tune of "Frère Jacques.")

> Two tigers, two tigers,
> Quickly run, quickly run.
> One does not have ears; the other has no tail.
> Very strange! Very strange!

At the end of the song, the player drops the tiger tail behind another player. The chosen student chases the tail dropper back to his or her place. The last one to sit down is the next tail dropper!

Queenie, Queenie

In this game from England, a girl is picked to be Queenie (or a boy is picked to be Kingie). The rest of the players stand several feet away from Queenie. Queenie turns her back to the group and throws the ball over her shoulder. The player who gets the ball hides it behind his or her back. The rest of the group also put their hands behind their backs. Queenie then turns around, and everyone shouts in rhythm:

> Queenie, Queenie, who's got the ball?
> Are they short, or are they tall?
> Are they hairy, or are they bald?
> You don't know because you don't have the ball!

Queenie guesses who has the ball. If she's wrong, the person with the ball becomes the next Queenie (or Kingie). If she's right, she repeats the game.

Zippity Zydeco!

Zydeco is a style of party music best known in southern Louisiana. French-speaking people were the first to make this music. Zydeco mixes sounds from Creole, Cajun, and Caribbean music with African American blues and jazz.

The two most important instruments in zydeco music are the **accordion** and the **rubboard.**

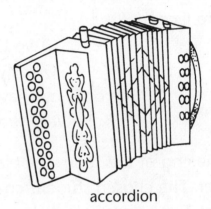

accordion

The first zydeco musicians played the button accordion, or squeezebox. Today they use the piano accordion.

Long ago zydeco musicians played washboards like the one your great-great-great-grandmother used to wash clothes—a musician would hang it on a rope around the neck. Later a musician made an apron washboard out of metal. This is called a rubboard, or *frottoir.*

rubboard

You can play zydeco rhythms, too! Pick a rhythm instrument, and play these rhythms.

Zydeco   Blues   Waltz

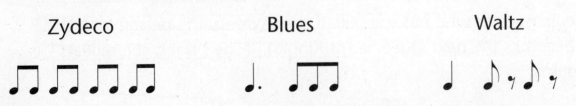

Mid-Unit Review

1. Circle the dotted half notes. Draw a square around the treble cleft(s). Draw a triangle around the dotted quarter note(s).

2. Circle the eighth notes. Draw a square around the quarter note(s). Draw a triangle around the quarter note rest(s).

3. Draw a line from the word to what it means.

a. ritando   a five-note scale: *do-re-mi-so-la*

b. pentatonic   speed up

c. accelerando   slow down

4. Write a pentatonic scale using dotted quarter notes.

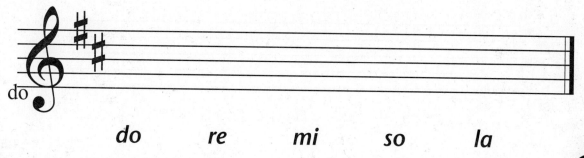

do   re   mi   so   la

Pitching the Poem

Use the pitches of the pentatonic scale to set the frog poem to music. Write a ♩ note for every word; give "little" and "isn't" two pitches each.

la
so
mi
re
do

Do you want my lit-tle frog?

la
so
mi
re
do

Could you please house and feed him?

la
so
mi
re
do

It is-n't that he is-n't nice.

la
so
mi
re
do

I guess I just don't need him!

Name _____ Date _____

Dixieland Instruments

Cut out the pictures of Dixieland band instruments.

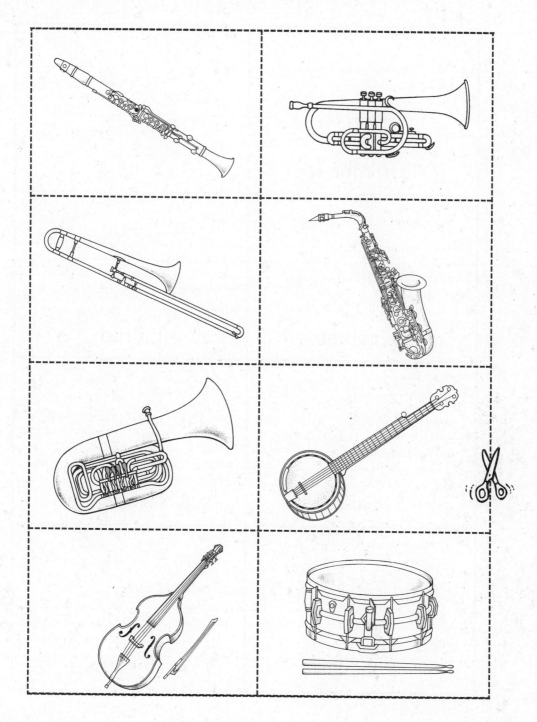

Name _____ Date _____

Dixieland Instruments

Paste each Dixieland instrument in the correct box.

1. trombone	2. tuba
3. cornet	4. drum
5. clarinet	6. saxophone
7. banjo	8. string bass

Spotlight Your Success!

Review
Circle the correct answer.

1. Which pattern shows *do re mi so la?*

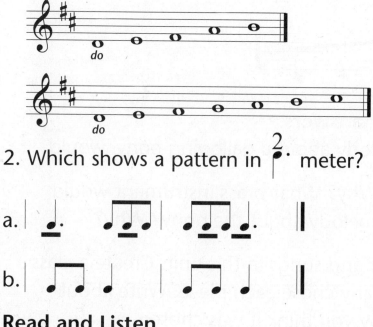

2. Which shows a pattern in $\frac{2}{4}$ meter?

Read and Listen

Read these patterns, then listen to identify.

1. Which pattern is in $\frac{2}{4}$ meter?

a.

b.

Spotlight Your Success!

 RESOURCE MASTER 5•11

2. **Listen** to these patterns. Which uses *do re mi so la?*

a.

do

b.

do

Think! Write or tell your answers.

1. If you composed a melody about a galloping pony, would you use $\frac{2}{4}$ or $\frac{2}{8}$· meter? Why? What brass instrument would you choose to play your melody about the pony? Why?

2. List your favorite music and songs in this unit. Create a class graph that shows how many chose each piece. Write about the favorite piece and why you think it was chosen.

Create and Perform

In groups, create a performance of "The Elephant Carries a Great Big Trunk," with a narrator, movement, and instruments.

Tell:

- Your choice of rhythms.
- Your choice of instruments.
- Things you did well and those that need work.

Perform your piece.

 78

Name _____ Date _____

Self-Assessment

Who worked with you on the unit project?
Write everyone's name.

_____   _____

_____   _____

What did you like best about the project? _____

_____

If you could do the project again, what would you change?

_____

How did your group do during the performance?
The goals for the project are listed below.
Put an X in the box that shows how you did.

Goal	😀	🙂	😐	🙁
The rhythm worked well with the melody.				
The melody matched the poem's meaning.				
When the music got louder or softer, it matched the poem's meaning.				
When the music went faster or slower, it matched the poem's meaning.				

Name _____   Date _____

Teacher Assessment

	Melody	Dynamics and Tempo	Rhythm
Excellent	The melody expressed and enhanced the meaning of the words.	The dynamics and tempo expressed and intensified the meaning of the words.	The rhythm was original and enhanced the melody.
*Competent	The melody expressed the meaning of the words.	The dynamics and tempo expressed the meaning of the words.	The rhythm was original and complimented the melody.
Progressing	The melody sometimes expressed the meaning of the words.	The dynamics and tempo expressed the meaning of the words most of the time.	The rhythm was original but did not relate to the melody.
Showing Little Progress	The melody rarely expressed the meaning of the words.	The dynamics and tempo expressed the meaning of the words some of the time.	The rhythm duplicated that of the poem.

Not Scorable: Did not participate.

*Competent is the expected level for all students.

USE WITH GRADE 2, UNIT 5, CREATIVE UNIT PROJECT

School-to-Home Letter

Dear Family,

As we approach spring, students in music class are learning songs about gardening and things that grow. Ask your child to sing (just for you) a song from music class. These private, casual performances help build confidence in even the shyest of children. Be sure to sing along if you know the song.

In Unit 6 your child is continuing to learn about rhythm patterns in the time signature $\frac{2}{4}$ or $\frac{6}{8}$ time. Help your child identify the meter in spoken language, as well. For example, in $\frac{6}{8}$ time a three-syllable word such as *strawberry* follows the rhythmic pattern of three eighth notes ♪♪♪; a two-syllable word like *carrot* follows the pattern of quarter note, eighth note ♩ ♪; and a one-syllable word like *corn* has one beat ♩.

Your child will also continue to work with the pitches *do, re, mi, so,* and *la* and learn to identify steps, skips, and leaps in music. Sing with your child, and help him or her hear when two pitches are right next to each other in the scale (a step), when they skip over one pitch, and when they leap over two or more pitches.

This unit also introduces students to the four instrument families of the orchestra: woodwinds, brass, strings, and percussion. When you and your child listen to orchestral music, ask him or her which instrument family or families are playing. What specific instruments can your child hear? To what family does each of these instruments belong?

In this unit your child will learn some folk songs from a variety of places, including Mexico, Korea, the United States, and the Hopi Indian nation. He or she will listen to music from an opera called *The Barber of Seville,* study a musical form called *rondo,* and listen to the music of Ludwig van Beethoven. This summer, try to keep music alive for your child. Continue exposing him or her to as many musical experiences as possible.

Sincerely,

Second Grade Music Teacher

School-to-Home Letter

Estimada Familia:

A medida que nos acercamos a la primavera, los alumnos de la clase de música aprenden canciones sobre la jardinería y sobre las cosas que crecen. Pida a su hijo que cante (sólo para usted) una canción de la clase de música. Estas actuaciones privadas, informales, ayudan a construir la confianza hasta en los niños más tímidos. Cante con su hijo si sabe la canción.

En la Unidad 6 su hijo continúa aprendiendo sobre esquemas de ritmo dentro de la armadura de tiempos ♩., o de ⁶⁄₈. Ayude a su hijo a identificar la métrica en el lenguaje hablado también. Por ejemplo, en tiempo de ⁶⁄₈ una palabra de tres sílabas como *frutilla* sigue el esque-ma rítmico de tres corcheas ♪♪♪ ; una palabra de dos sílabas como *casa* sigue el esquema de negra, corchea ♩ ♪ ; y una palabra de una sílaba como *pez* tiene un compás ♩.

Su hijo también continuará trabajando con los tonos *do, re, mi, sol* y *la* y aprenderá a identificar los tonos, saltos y pasos en la música. Cante con su hijo y ayúdelo a escuchar cuando dos tonos están uno al lado del otro en la escala (un tono), cuando éstos saltan sobre un tono (nota) y cuando pasan saltando sobre dos o más tonos (notas).

Esta unidad también les presenta a los alumnos las cuatro familias de instrumentos de la orquesta: vientos de madera, metales (brass), cuerdas y percusión. Cuando usted y su hijo escuchen musical orquestal, pregúntele qué familia o familias de instrumento están tocando. ¿Qué instrumentos específicos puede oír su hijo? ¿A qué familia pertenece cada uno de los instrumentos?

En esta unidad su hijo aprenderá algunas canciones *folk* de varios lugares, incluyendo México, Corea, los Estados Unidos y la nación de los indios Hopi. Su hijo escuchará música de una ópera llamada *El barbero de Sevilla,* estudiará un esquema musical llamada *rondó,* y escuchará la música de Ludwig van Beethoven. Este verano trate de mantener viva la música para su hijo o hija. Haga que tenga tantas experiencias musicales como sea posible.

Atentamente,

Maestra de Música de Segundo Grado

Creative Unit Project

RESOURCE MASTER 6•2

For this project, you will work with one other student to build a song with words, rhythm, and melody. You will join your song with another pair's song for a performance.

STEP 1 (after Lesson 1)
Decide on a topic for your song. What do you and your partner enjoy? Do you like sports, sea life, weather? After you have decided on a topic, list some words that you would use to describe it.

_____

_____

Now choose and circle your favorite words on the list. How could you create rhythms that would help show the word meanings? Create an 8-beat rhythm pattern for $\frac{2}{4}$ below.

- Start with these three rhythm building blocks. Each one is one beat in $\frac{2}{4}$ Which patterns work with the words you have chosen? Try out different patterns until the words and rhythms work well together.

- Notate your final rhythm pattern. Write one beat in each square below.

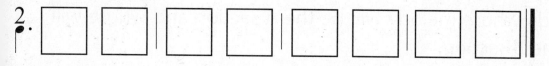

- Pick a rhythm instrument, and practice playing your rhythm.

Creative Unit Project

RESOURCE MASTER 6•3

STEP 2 (after Lesson 2)

Write a melody for the rhythm you have made up. Use *do, re, mi, so,* and *la.* Begin and end on *do.*

- Here are the pitches and where they go on the staff.

- Write your final melody on the staff below. Practice singing and playing your melody.

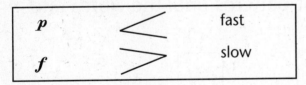

STEP 3 (after Lesson 3)

Now work on putting some feelings into your song. Practice with the following musical elements. When you like how something sounds, add the marking to your music.

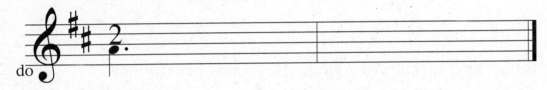

STEP 4 (after Lesson 4)

Work with another pair of students to create a song in ABA form. Combine your two songs.

- Decide whose melody will be the A section and whose will be the B section.
- Practice your ABA composition. Work hard on pitch, rhythm, and expression. Then play it for the class.

Garden Rhythms

The rhythm in the rain is helping this garden grow! Pick the name of a fruit or vegetable to go with each rhythm pattern. Cut out the pictures, and paste them next to their matching rhythms. Clap each rhythm. Then say the names of your plants in rhythm to a friend.

Corn

Strawberry

Pineapple

Spinach

Carrot

Beet

Pitching a Puppy Poem

Each verse of the poem "Bliss" has two rhymes. The ends of lines one and four form rhyme A, and the ends of lines two and three form rhyme B. This makes the rhyme pattern ABBA. Create two melodies to go with this pattern. Make each melody four beats. Use *do, re, mi,* and *so* for the pitches. Use one melody for the A rhymes and the other melody for the B rhymes. Then sing your song.

Name _____ Date _____

Animal Rhythms

The animals have escaped! Get the zoo animals back in their cages by matching their names to a rhythm. Cut them out and paste them above a matching rhythm. (Look for other clues, too.) When the animals are all in their cages, read their names together in rhythm.

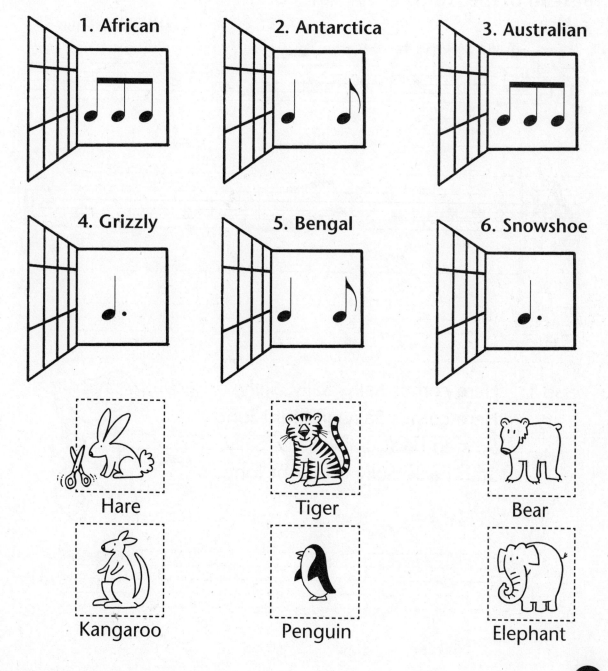

1. African

2. Antarctica

3. Australian

4. Grizzly

5. Bengal

6. Snowshoe

Hare

Tiger

Bear

Kangaroo

Penguin

Elephant

Pitching "Here Comes Sally"

In the song below, "Here Comes Sally," write the pitch name under each note. (If the notes are tied together, you only need to write the pitch name one time.) Use the pitch names instead of the words to sing the song.

African American Folk Song

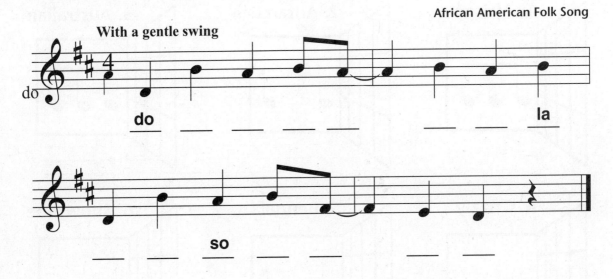

Verse 1:   Here comes Sally, Sally, Sally,
            Here comes Sally all night long.
            So step back, Sally, Sally, Sally.
            Step back, Sally, all night long.

USE WITH GRADE 2, UNIT 6, LESSON 4

Mid-Unit Review

Below is the last half of "Animal Fair," but that silly monkey took the black out of most of the notes. Color the notes. Use blue for *do*, yellow for *mi*, red for *so*, and green for *la*. Circle this rhythm pattern: ♩ ♪ Draw a square around this pattern ♫♫ Draw a triangle around the dotted quarter notes ♩.

Instrument Families   RESOURCE MASTER   6•9

Color and cut out these pictures of different instruments.

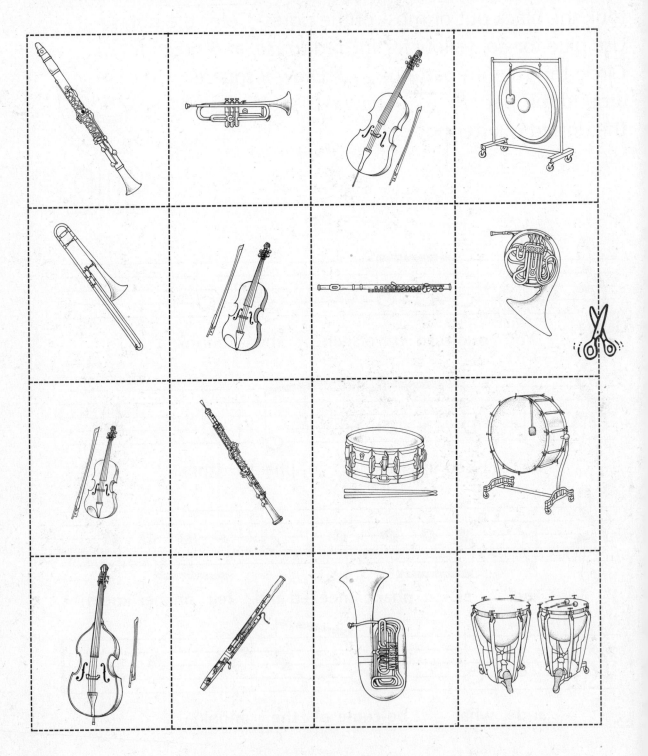

Name _____ Date _____

Instrument Families

Paste each instrument in the box beside its family name.

Strings

Brass

Woodwinds

Percussion

Steps, Skips, and Leaps

Many kinds of trees grow in a rainforest. Some of the trees are very tall. Some of the trees are shorter.

Your teacher will play two notes. Circle the shortest tree if it is a step. Circle the middle tree if it is a skip. Circle the tallest tree if it is a leap.

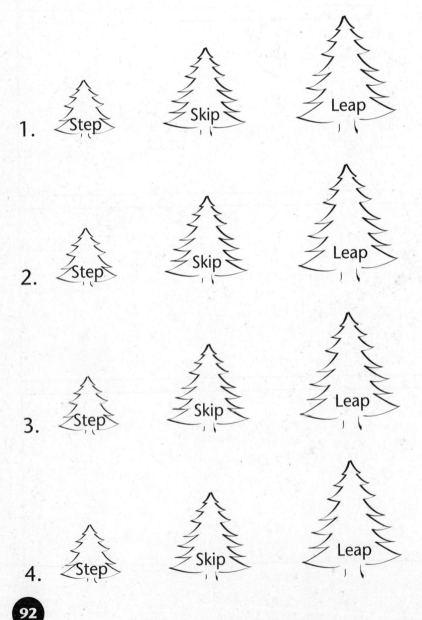

1. Step   Skip   Leap

2. Step   Skip   Leap

3. Step   Skip   Leap

4. Step   Skip   Leap

Name _____ Date _____

Spotlight Your Success!

Review
Circle the correct answer.

1. Which shows the pitches in a pentatonic scale?

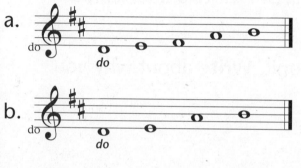

a.

b.

2. Which rhythm shows three sounds to a beat in $\frac{2}{}$?

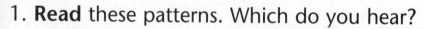

a. ♩ ♩ ♩   b. ♩♫   c. ♩ ♩ ♩

Read and Listen
Circle the correct answer.

1. **Read** these patterns. Which do you hear?

a.

b.

2. **Read** these patterns. Which do you hear?

a.

b.

Spotlight Your Success!

Think! Write or tell your answers.

1. Tell what an aria is and how it is different from a folk song.

2. Name the four instrument families. Pick two and tell how they are alike and different.

3. Choose a song you like in this unit. **Write** about why you like it.

Create and Perform

1. **Create** a pattern two measures long.

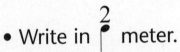

- Write in $\frac{2}{4}$ meter.
- Use only *so* and *la.*

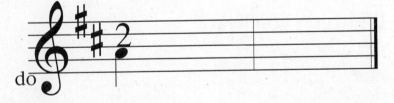

2. Play your pattern as you sing "All Around the Buttercup."

Name _____ Date _____

Self-Assessment

Who was your partner? _____

_____

What other two students did you and your partner work with?

_____   _____

What did you like best about the project? _____

_____

If you could do the project again, what would you change?

_____

How did your group do during the performance?
The goals for the project are listed below.
Put an X in the box that best answers the question.

Goal	😁	🙂	😐	🙁
We performed with energy and enjoyed doing it.				
Our music matched the meaning of the words.				
We followed the song's form and markings.				

Name _____ Date _____

Teacher Assessment   RESOURCE MASTER   6•13

	Performance with energy, focus, and confidence	Music reflecting the meaning of the words	Performance following dynamic and tempo markings
Excellent	Consistently performed with energy, focus, and confidence.	Music reflected and helped to interpret the meaning of the words.	Consistently performed markings.
*Competent	Generally performed with energy, focus, and confidence.	Music reflected the meaning of the words.	Generally performed markings.
Progressing	Occasionally performed with energy, focus, and confidence.	Music partially reflected the meaning of the words.	Occasionally performed markings.
Showing Little Progress	Infrequently performed with energy, focus, and confidence.	Music did not reflect the meaning of the words.	Infrequently performed markings.

Not Scorable: Did not participate.

*Competent is the expected level for all students.

Writing Rhythms

Practice writing some notes. Fill them in.

Make up your own rhythm. Write 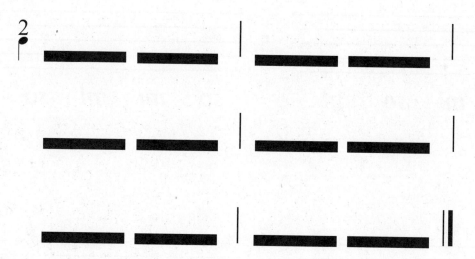 or ♫ above each beat bar. Then clap the rhythm.

Writing *So* and *Mi*

Write *so* and *mi* pitches below. The first one is done for you.

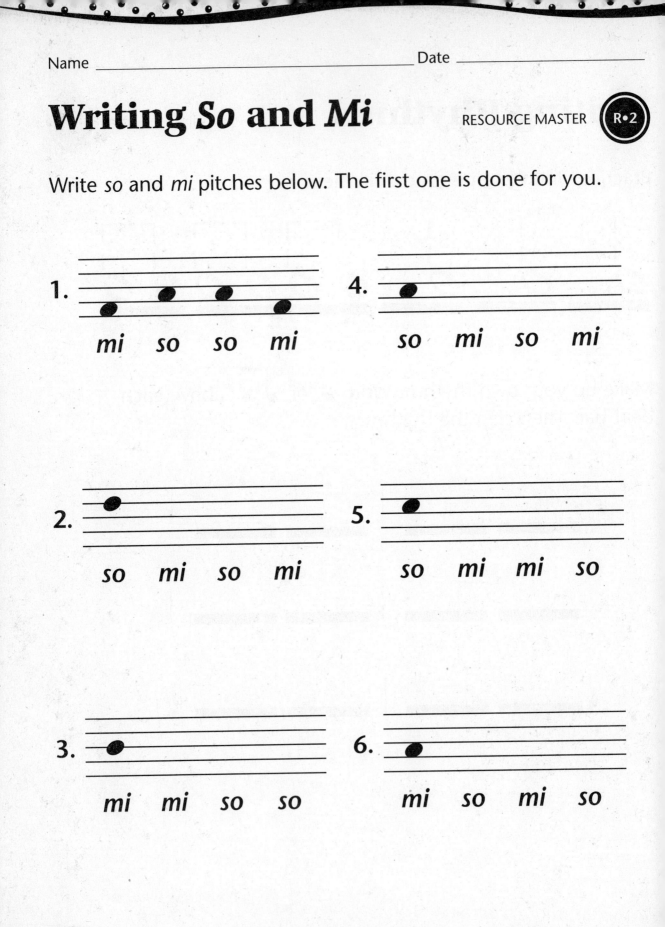

1. mi   so   so   mi

2. so   mi   so   mi

3. mi   mi   so   so

4. so   mi   so   mi

5. so   mi   mi   so

6. mi   so   mi   so

Mi, So and Quarter Rests

1. Use a red and blue marker or crayon. Color the note heads of each *so* red. Color the note heads of each *mi* blue. Sing the song using *so* and *mi* when you are finished.

Hey, Hey, Look at Me

American Singing Game
Words Adapted by MMH

2. Circle each quarter rest. Choose an instrument and play each rhythm.

A Melody with Mi and So

Pick games from the painting *Children's Games* by Pieter Brueghel as words for your song. A list of the games is in your book on p. 247.

Create a song using *mi* and *so* and the game rhythms in your book. Write the words under the music.

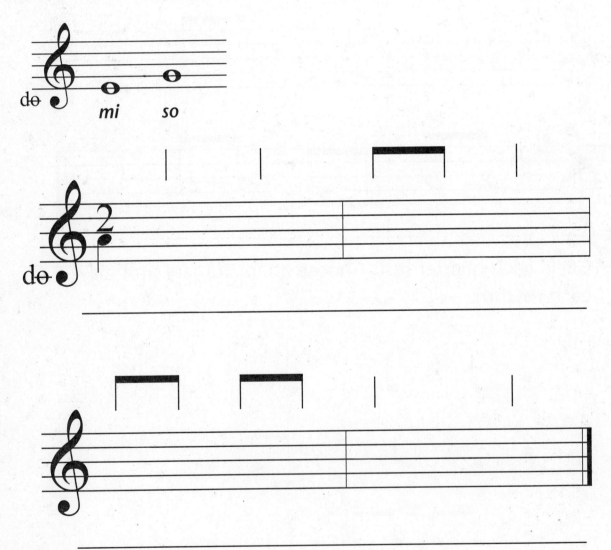

Finding *Mi, So,* and *La*

1. Circle *la* in the song each time you see it. Draw a box around each *so.* Draw a line under each *mi.*

Plainsies, Clapsies

American Folk Song

Plain - sies,   clap - sies,   twirl a - round to   back - sies,

Right hand,   left   hand,   stretch it   high,   stoop it   low,

Touch your knee, touch your toe, touch your heel and 'round you go.

2. Sing "Plainsies, Clapsies" using *mi, so,* and *la.* Then sing the song with the words.

Identifying *So, Mi, and La*

Fill in the blanks under the notes with *so, mi,* or *la*. Draw a box around the two *mi-la* skips.

Red Rover

American Singing Game

Quarter Rests and *Mi, So,* and *La*

Fill in the blanks under the notes with *so, mi,* or *la*.
Then circle the quarter rests.

Eating Lizards

Carol Huffman

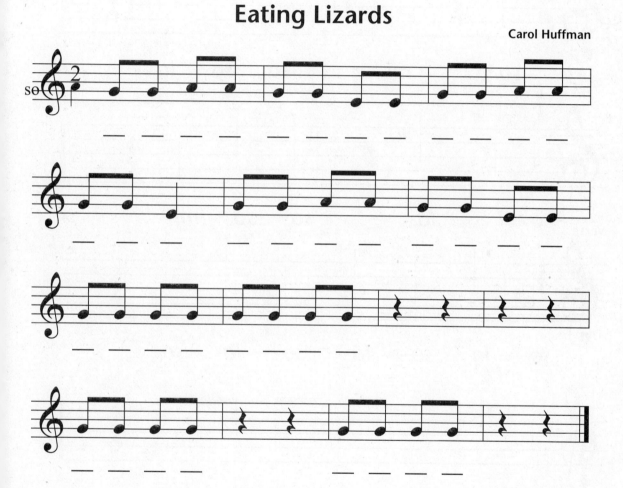

Clap the rhythm of the song.
Sing the song using *mi, so,* and *la.*

Riddle Song

Draw the missing note heads. Circle the quarter rests.

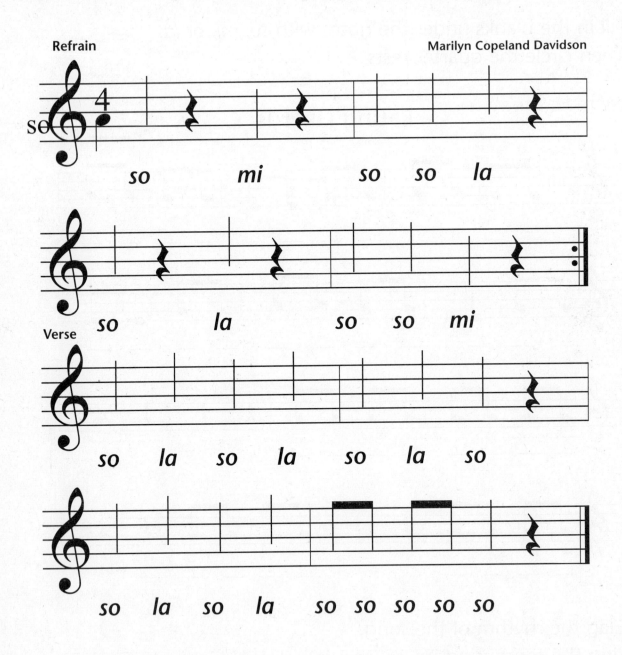

Refrain

Marilyn Copeland Davidson

so   mi   so   so   la

so   la   so   so   mi

Verse

so   la   so   la   so   la   so

so   la   so   la   so   so   so   so   so

Writing Rhythms

Copy the rhythm patterns that your teacher has written on the board.

Use Rhythm Pattern 3 as an ostinato with "Who Has the Penny?"

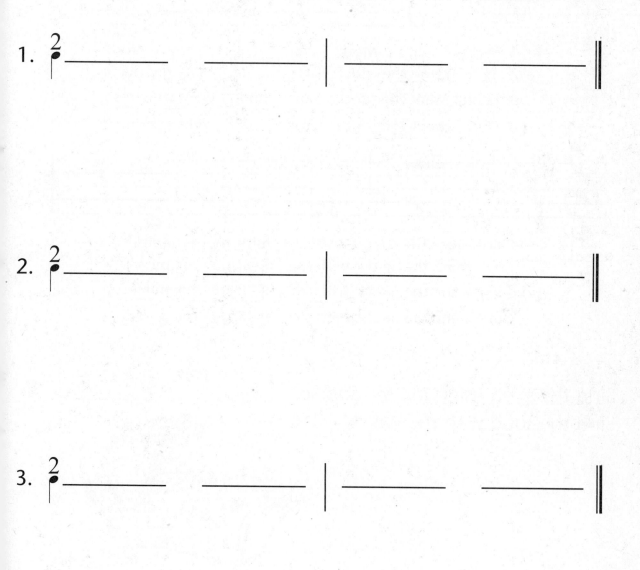

Do, Mi, and So

Use a red, blue, and yellow crayon or marker. Color each *do* yellow. Color each *mi* red. Color each *so* blue.

Mother, Mother

American Jump Rope Game

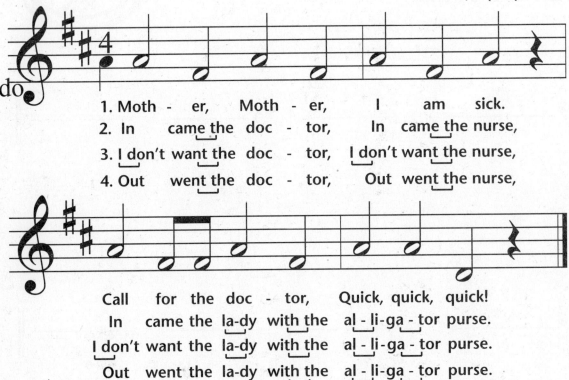

1. Moth - er,   Moth - er,   I   am   sick.
2. In   came the doc - tor,   In   came the nurse,
3. I don't want the doc - tor,   I don't want the nurse,
4. Out   went the doc - tor,   Out went the nurse,

Call   for   the doc - tor,   Quick, quick, quick!
In   came the la-dy with the   al - li-ga - tor purse.
I don't want the la-dy with the   al - li-ga - tor purse.
Out   went the la-dy with the   al - li-ga - tor purse.

Sing the song using *do*, *mi*, and *so*.
Sing the song with the words.

Finding *La*

Find *la* in the song "Daisy Chain." Cut out the hand sign for *la* at the bottom of the page, and paste it above *la* in the song.

Daisy Chain

American Singing Game

Chain, chain, dai - sy chain,

All the pret - ty flow - ers,

One for you, and one for me, and

one for Jen - ny Bow - ers.

Composing with Do, Mi, So, and La

do mi so la

Write a new melody, using the rhythm of line 1 of "Donkey, Donkey." Use the pitches *do, mi, so,* and *la,* writing them in the correct place on the staff. Write each pitch below each rhythm notation above the staff.

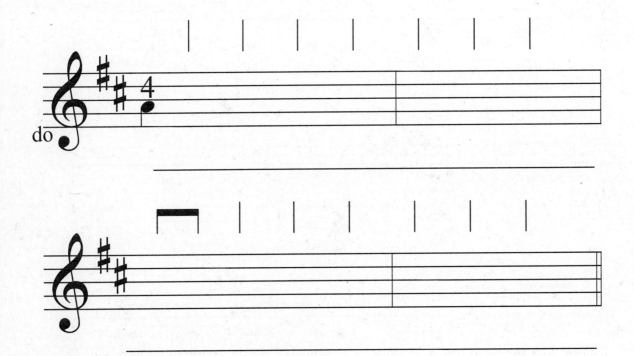

Add words for your new melody.

More *Do, Mi, So,* and *La*

RESOURCE MASTER R•13

Write *do, mi, so,* or *la* in the blanks below the frog notes.

Mr. Frog

American Singing Game

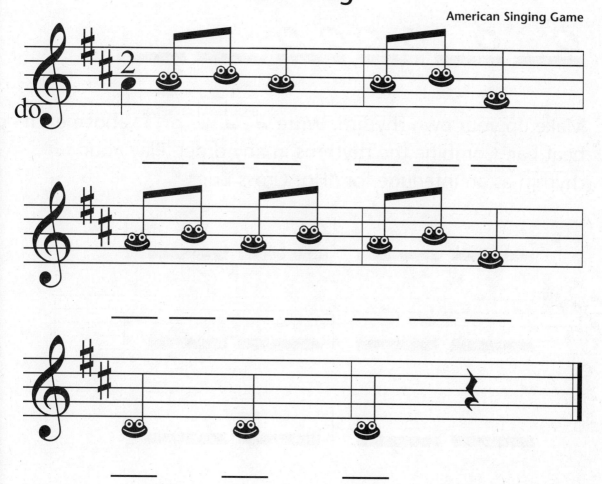

Sing the song using *do, mi, so,* and *la.*

Practicing Quarter Notes, RESOURCE MASTER R•14
Eighth Notes, and Quarter Rests

1. Practice writing notes and rests.

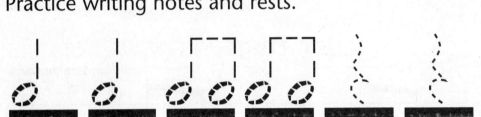

2. Make up your own rhythm. Write ♩ ♫ or 𝄽 above each beat bar. Combine the rhythms in any order. Play your rhythm as an interlude for "Hot Cross Buns."

Rhythms with *Mi, Re,* and *Do*

1. Write *do, re,* or *mi* on the lines below the notes.

___ ___ ___ ___   ___ ___ ___ ___ ___

2. Make your own rhythm stew. Write ♩ ♫ or 𝄽 on the blanks. Then clap your rhythm.

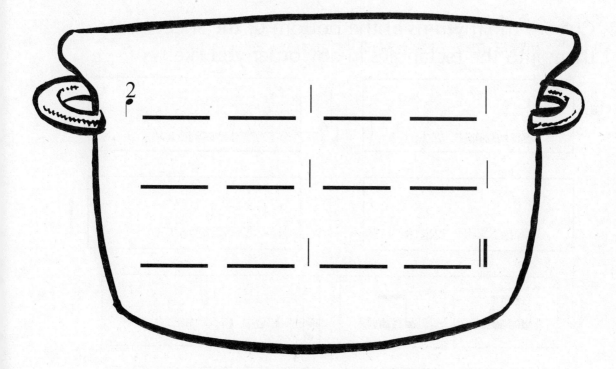

Do, Re, Mi, and So

1. Write *re, mi,* or *so* in the blanks on the stairs.

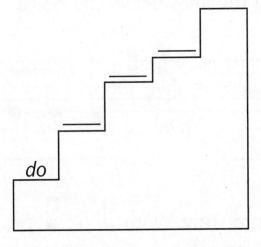

do

2. Cut out the rhythms at the bottom of the sheet. Paste them into the rectangles in any order you like.

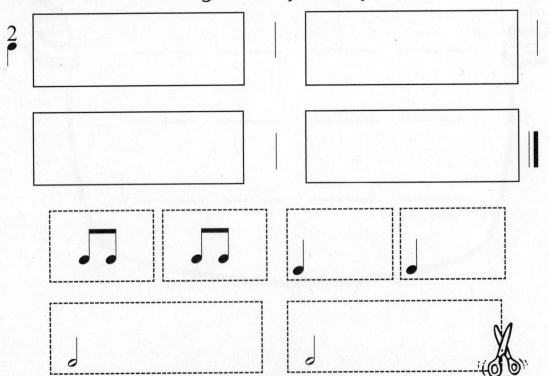

Pitches and Half Notes

1. Draw the missing note heads.

Matarile

Mexican Folk Song

do   do   re   mi   do   do   re   re   so   so   mi   do

do   do   re   mi   do   do   re   re   so   so   do

2. Solve the following rhythm math problems. Use ♩ ♩ ♩. or ♫ for your answers.

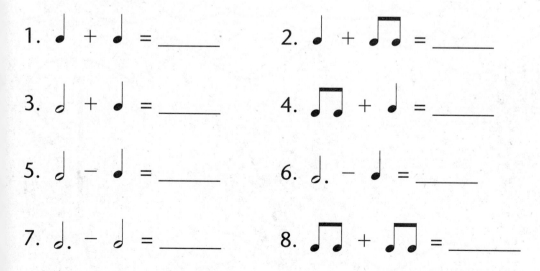

1. ♩ + ♩ = _____   2. ♩ + ♫ = _____

3. ♩ + ♩ = _____   4. ♫ + ♩ = _____

5. ♩ − ♩ = _____   6. ♩. − ♩ = _____

7. ♩. − ♩ = _____   8. ♫ + ♫ = _____

Dotted Half Notes

Draw a circle around each *do*. Draw a line under each *re*.
Draw a box around each *mi*.

Each box below contains a rhythmic pattern that has three
beats. Use the notes in the boxes to compose your own
rhythm. The rhythms in each box will fill one measure. Use
each rhythmic pattern.

Finding *Do, Re, Mi, So,* and *La*

Write the pitch syllable name under each note in "Here Comes a Bluebird." Remember that when *do* is in a space, *mi* and *so* are in spaces too.

Here Comes a Bluebird

American Singing Game

Here   comes   a   blue - bird

in   through   my   win - dow,

Hey,   did - dle - um - a

day,   day,   day.

Pentatonic Pitches

RESOURCE MASTER R•20

Compose a melody using *do, re, mi, so,* and *la.* Use the rhythm patterns under the staff for your melody. **Use *do* for your starting and ending pitch.**

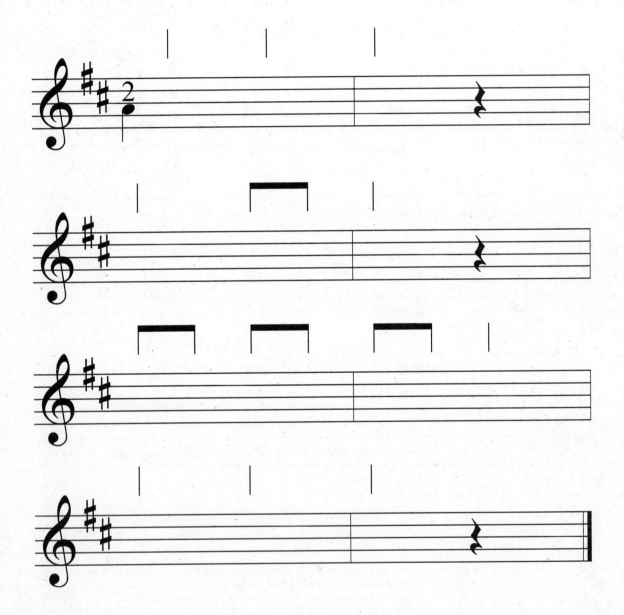

More *Do, Re, Mi, So,* and *La*

Fill in the empty measures in "Knock the Cymbals" below. Notice that *do* is now in the first space. Use the rhythms shown above the measures.

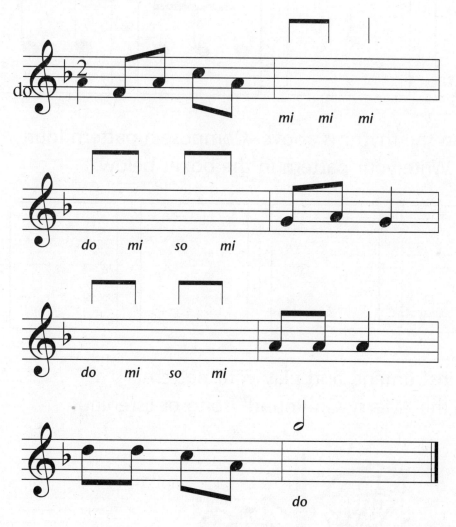

Sing the melody of the song with pitch syllables.

Then sing the song with the words, and raise a hand whenever you sing the *do mi so mi* pattern.

Patterns in $\frac{2}{\bullet}$ Meter

Here are rhythms in $\frac{2}{\bullet}$ meter.

Choose from the rhythms above. Compose a pattern four beats long. Write your pattern in the boxes below.

 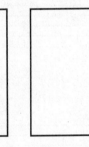 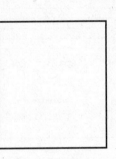 

Choose an instrument, and play your pattern.
Play it with the "Merry-Go-Round" song or listening.

Rhythms in 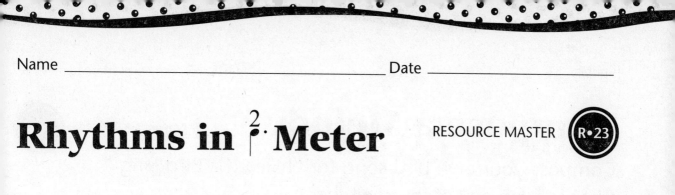 Meter

Each of the patterns below has one beat in ⅔· time.

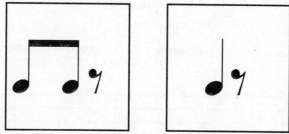

Compose your own rhythm using the patterns above. Use two patterns in each measure. Name your rhythm.

The title of my piece is "_____."

Clap your rhythm.

Choose an instrument, and play your rhythm.

Compose a Melody

RESOURCE MASTER R•24

Compose your own bird song for "I Heard a Bird Sing."
Choose from any of these pitches.

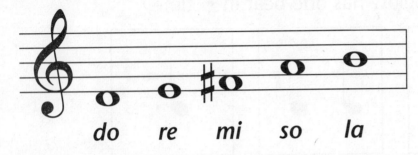

do   re   mi   so   la

Write one pitch above each syllable. Add the rhythms you see above the line.

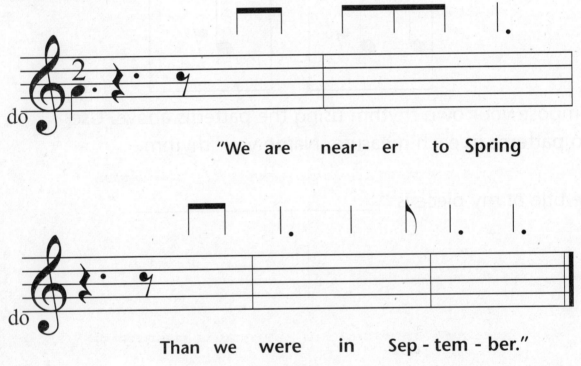

"We are   near - er   to Spring

Than we   were   in   Sep - tem - ber."

Sing or play your new melody!

Beat Bars

▬▬ ▬▬ ▬▬ ▬▬

▬▬ ▬▬ ▬▬ ▬▬

▬▬ ▬▬ ▬▬ ▬▬

▬▬ ▬▬ ▬▬ ▬▬

Name _____ Date _____

Pitch Ladder

Curwen Hand Signs

do

ti

la

so

fa

mi

re

do

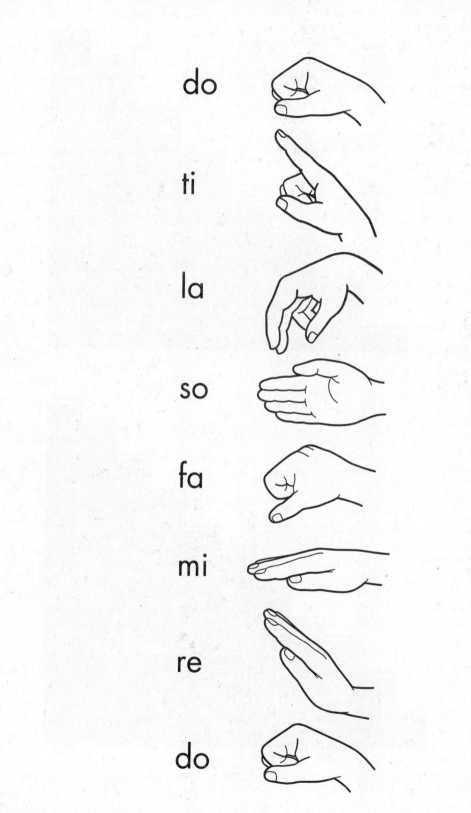

Pitch Stairs

Name _____ Date _____

Pitch Xylophone

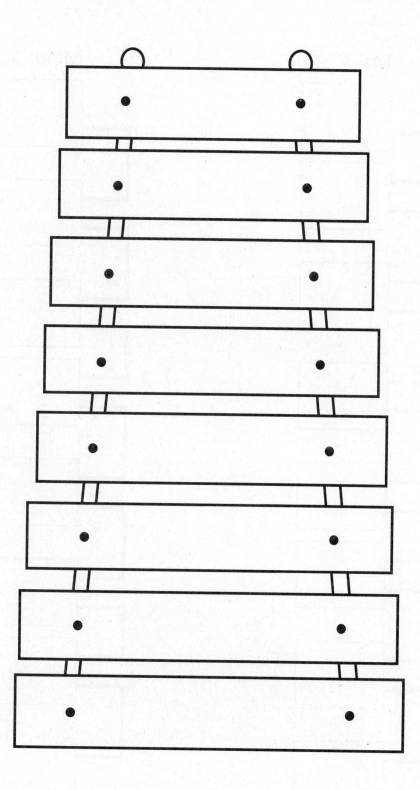

Scale Brackets

Major Scale

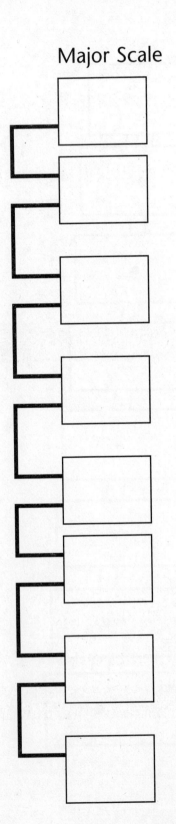

Minor Scale

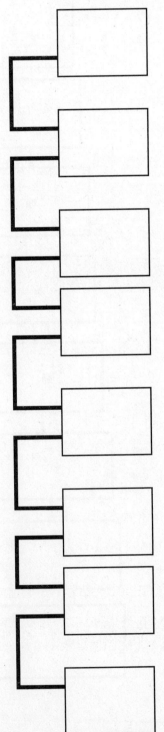

Name _____ Date _____

Seussical Junior

Based on the works of Dr. Seuss
Music by Stephen Flaherty
Lyrics by Lynn Ahrens
Book by Lynn Ahrens and Stephen Flaherty
Co-Conceived by Lynn Ahrens, Stephen Flaherty, and Eric Idle

NARRATOR: It's great to learn something new and exciting
So we'd like to present something fun and inviting;
With rhymes running wild and out on the loose,
Of course they were written by—who?

KIDS: DR. SEUSS!

Song 1: Oh, The Thinks You Can Think!

ALL: Oh, the Thinks you can think!
Oh, the Thinks you can think
If you're willing to try.

Think invisible ink!
Or a Gink with a stink!
Or a stair to the sky!

If you open your mind,
Oh, the Thinks you will find lining up to get loose . . .

Oh, the Thinks you can think when you think about Seuss!

End of Song

NARRATOR: *(To the KIDS.)*
We'll take a few stories and cook up a stew.
Which Dr. Seuss story would you like to do?

KIDS (Group 1): "If I Ran the Zoo."

KIDS (Group 2): Or "Solla Sollew."

KIDS (Group 3): How about Horton who heard the small Who?

NARRATOR: "Horton Hears a Who!" is a great idea.

KIDS: HURRAY!

(NARRATOR reads from the book.)

NARRATOR: On the eleventh of May
In the Jungle of Nool
In the heat of the day
In the cool of the pool
He was splashing

KIDS: Splash!

NARRATOR: Enjoying the jungle's great joys
When Horton the Elephant
Heard a small noise.

KID 1: Help! Help!

NARRATOR: So Horton stopped splashing.
He looked toward the sound.
"That's funny," thought Horton,
"There's no one around."
Then he heard it again! Just a very faint yelp
As if some tiny person were calling for help.

KID 2: Help! Help!

NARRATOR: "I'll help you," said Horton,
"But who are you, and where?"
He looked and he looked.
He could see nothing there
But a small speck of dust
Blowing past, through the air.

"I say! How confusing! I've never
Of a small speck of dust that is able to yell.
So you know what I think? Why I think that there must
Be someone on top of that small speck of dust.
Some poor little person who's shaking with fear
That he'll blow in the pool!
He has no way to steer!"

KID 3: He's alone in the universe!

NARRATOR: And Horton the Elephant said:

Song 2: Horton Hears a Who

ALL: I'll just have to save him
Because after all,
A person's a person,
No matter how small.

A person's a person,
No matter how small.

End of Song

NARRATOR: So, gently, and using the greatest of care
The elephant stretched his great trunk in the air
And he lifted the dust speck and carried it over
And placed it down safe on a very soft clover.

KIDS: Thank you!

NARRATOR: I won't let you down. No, I won't let you fall.

Song 3: Horton Hears a Who Two

ALL: I'll just have to save him
Because after all,
A person's a person,
No matter how small.

A person's a person,
No matter how small.
Whoooo!

End of Song

NARRATOR: Now open your minds—you've got quite a tool
Let's all take a dive in McElligot's pool.

 130

ALL: This might be a pool,
Like I've read of in books,
Connected to one
Of those underground brooks!

An underground river
That starts here and flows
Right under the bathtub!

And then . . .

KID 4: Who knows?

ALL: It's possible.
Anything's possible!

It might go along
Down where no can see,
Right under State Highway
Two-Hundred-and-Three!

Right under the wagons!
Right under the toes of

KID 5: Missus Umbroso

ALL: Who's hanging out clothes!
It's possible.
Anything's possible!

This might be a river,
Now mightn't it be,

Connecting McElligot's pool
With the sea!

Then maybe some fish
Might be swimming,
Swimming toward me!

Oh, the sea is full
Of a number of fish.
If a fellow is patient,
He might get his wish!

And that's why I think
That I'm not such a fool
When I sit here and fish
In McElligot's pool.

It's possible.
Anything's possible!
It's possible.
Anything's possible!

End of Song

NARRATOR: What have we learned so far from Dr. Seuss?

KID 6: A person's a person, no matter how small.

KID 7: Anything's possible.

KID 8: I hate green eggs and ham?

NARRATOR: How did you learn that?
We haven't had green eggs and ham.

KIDS (GROUP 1): Let's have them now!

KIDS (GROUP 2): *(Pinching their noses.)* Yuck!

Song 5: Green Eggs and Ham

GROUP 2: I do not like green eggs and ham.
I do not like them Sam-I-Am.
I do not like them here or there.
I do not like them anywhere.

Not in a house.
Not with a mouse.
Not here or there.
Not anywhere.

I do not like green eggs and ham!
I do not like them, Sam-I-Am!

GROUP 1: Could you? Would you?
With a goat?
Could you? Would you?
On a boat?

Could you? Would you?
In the rain?
Could you? Would you?
On a train?

GROUP 2: Not with a goat. Not on a boat.
Not in the rain. Not on a train.
Not in a house. Not with a mouse.
Oh, no!

GROUP 1: Not in a box.

GROUP 2: Not with a fox.

GROUP 1: Not in a tree.

GROUP 2: You let me be!

ALL: I do not like green eggs and ham!
I do not like them Sam-I-Am!

End of Song

NARRATOR: *(To audience.)* That was a wonderful story, I say,
But that's all the time that we have for today.

All kinds of wonderful lessons were taught
Filling our thinkers with barrels of thought.

And just to be sure that his poetry sticks
Let's all sing a big Dr. Seuss Mega-Mix.

Song 6: Seussical Mega-Mix

ALL: Oh, the Thinks you can think!
Oh, the Thinks you can think if you're willing to try.

Think invisible ink!
Or a Gink with a stink!
Or a stair to the sky!

If you open your mind,
Oh, the Thinks you will find lining up to get loose . . .

Oh, the Thinks you can think
When you think about Seuss!

I'll just have to save him
Because, after all,
A person's a person,
No matter how small.

A person's a person,
No matter how small.

Oh, and that's why I think
That I'm not such a fool
When I sit here and fish
In McElligot's pool.

It's possible.
Anything's possible!

I do not like green eggs and ham.
I do not like them Sam-I-Am.
I do not like them here or there.
I do not like them anywhere.

Not in a house.
Not with a mouse.
Not here or there.
Not anywhere.

I do not like green eggs and ham!
I do not like them, Sam-I-Am!

Seuss! Seuss! Seuss!
I do not like green eggs and ham!

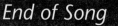

End of Song

Name _____ Date _____

City Traffic

Play the musical patterns below when you see the symbol in the poem.

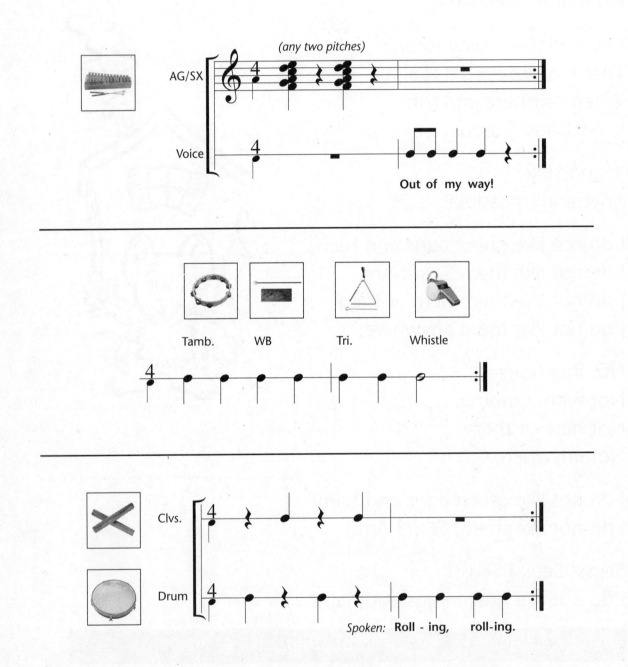

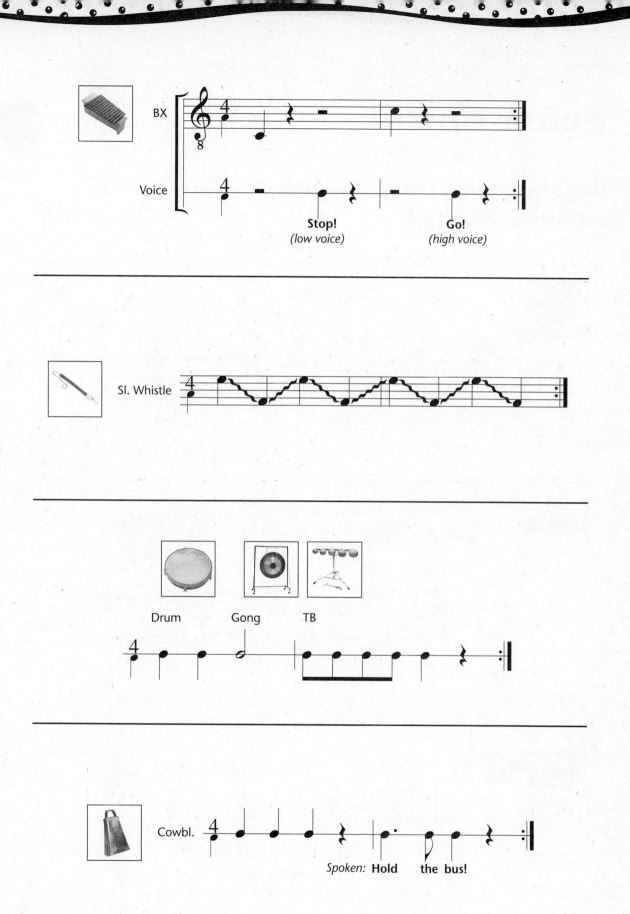

Señor Coyote

Play the musical patterns below when you see the symbol in the story.

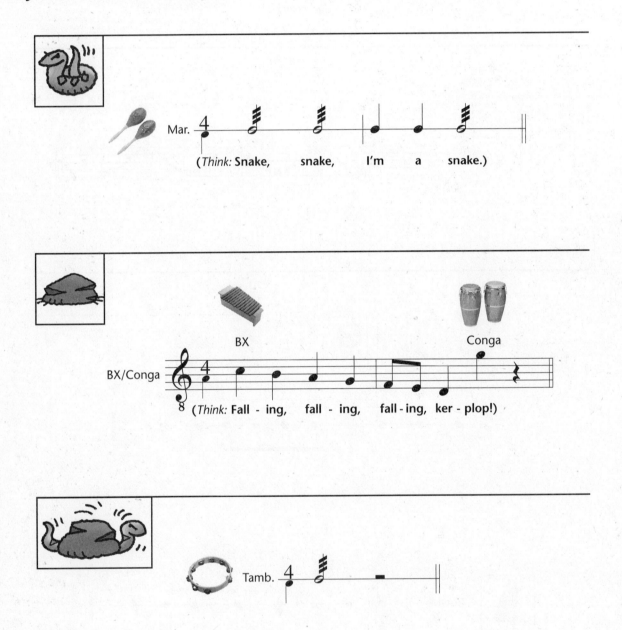

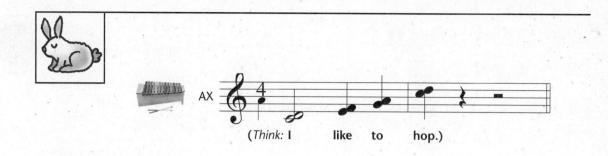

(*Think:* I   like   to   hop.)

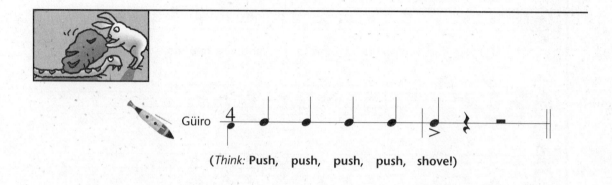

(*Think:* **Push,   push,   push,   push,   shove!**)

Ah - ooo!

If You Find You're in a Bind

Words and Music by
Cristi Cary Miller

The Drumming Spider

RESOURCE MASTER P•5

Play the musical patterns below when you see the symbol in the story.

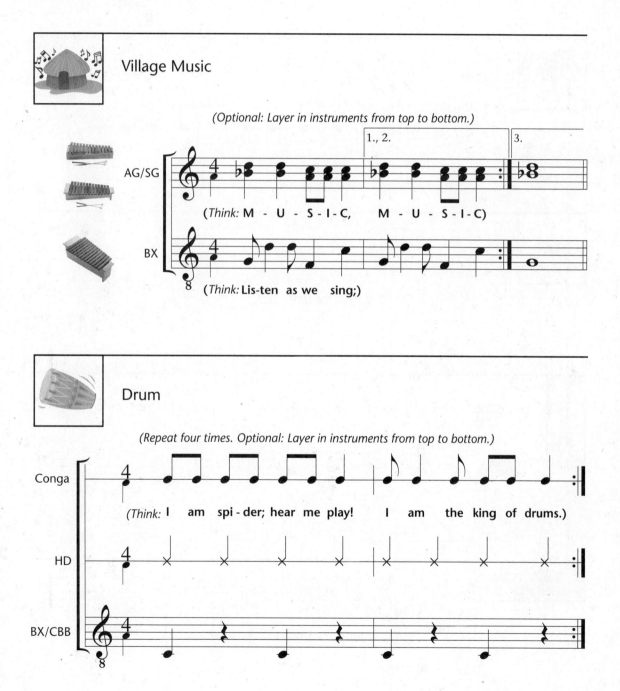

Village Music

(Optional: Layer in instruments from top to bottom.)

AG/SG

(Think: M – U – S – I – C, M – U – S – I – C)

BX

(Think: Lis-ten as we sing;)

Drum

(Repeat four times. Optional: Layer in instruments from top to bottom.)

Conga

(Think: I am spi-der; hear me play! I am the king of drums.)

HD

BX/CBB

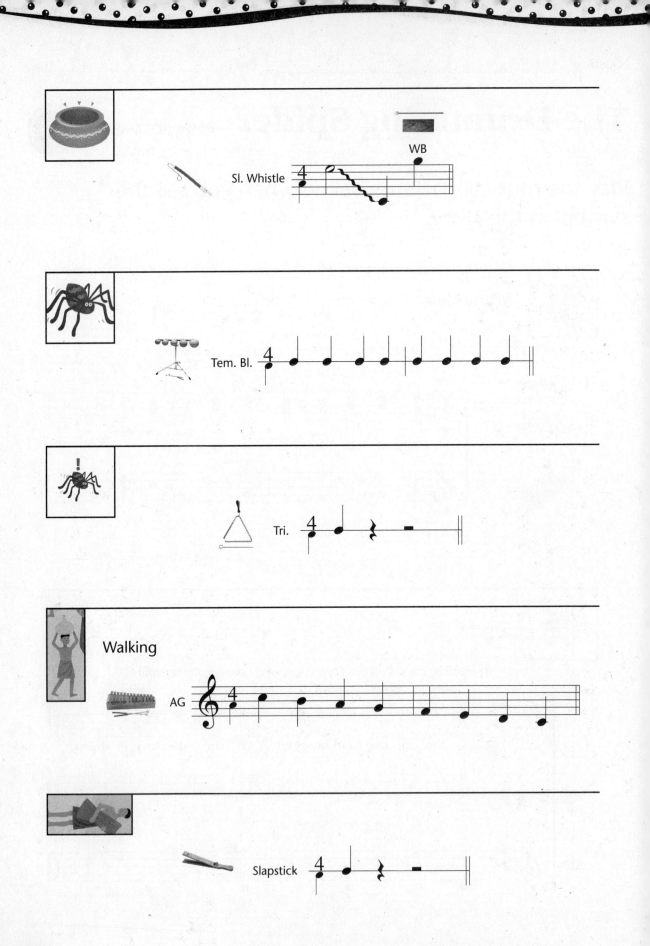

Name _____ Date _____

Spider King

Words and Music by
Cristi Cary Miller

Fall Apple Harvest

1. You can munch apples fresh and whole, or you can cook them in many different ways. Unscramble the letters to make words that show things you can make with apples.

a. I P E   __ __ __

b. C E I J U   __ __ __ __ __

c. U S A E C   __ __ __ __ __

d. T U T B E R   __ __ __ __ __ __

e. C D R I E   __ __ __ __ __

2. Do you know any other dishes made with apples?

Write your favorite apple dish on the line.

_____

3. Which is your favorite kind of apple?

Color the apple red, yellow, or green.

Name _____ Date _____

Columbus Day

Here are three tools used by Christopher Columbus.

 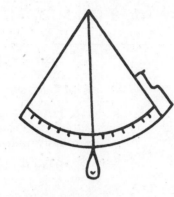 

A **compass**
shows direction:
north, south,
east, and west.

A **quadrant** is
useful if you are
using the stars
to steer.

A **sandglass** is
used to measure
time.

Color in the picture of Columbus. Choose one of the tools
above, and draw it in Columbus's hand or on the table.
Draw a hat on his head, as well!

Name _____ Date _____

Thanksgiving

Do you remember the song "Harvest" in which Emma gathered some sweet potatoes? Here's a tasty one-dish meal you can help to make for a fall supper!

1. Ask an adult to turn on the oven to **350°**. Let it warm up all the way!

2. Mash **2 pounds** of cooked **sweet potatoes** in a bowl.

3. Ask an adult to dice or cube **1/2 pound** of **ham**. Add it to the mashed sweet potatoes.

4. Add **1 can of corn** (drained) and **1/2 cup maple syrup**. Stir into the sweet potatoes and ham.

5. Beat **2 eggs** and **1/2 cup evaporated milk** together, and stir well into the sweet potato mixture.

6. Pour into a lightly greased 8-inch x 8-inch baking dish. If you wish, top with **marshmallows**, **walnuts**, or **pecans**.

7. Bake **45 to 60 minutes**. Ask an adult to test it with a knife in the center. When the knife comes out clean, it's time to eat!

While the dish is baking, teach your family the song "Thank You," using the words below. Sing it together before you eat!

Music by Franz Schubert

Thank You for the ma - ple sweet,

Sweet po - ta - toes, corn, and meat.

Thank You for the o - ven warm.

Thank You, God, for health and home.

USE WITH GRADE 2, SPOTLIGHT ON CELEBRATIONS

Name _____ Date _____

Hanukkah

1. Find the words listed below hidden in this puzzle. Look for words that read across, up and down, and diagonally.

H	A	P	L	A	Y	I	X	Y	H
O	M	I	W	I	N	D	O	W	A
G	L	E	E	S	G	F	Q	D	N
C	L	A	N	H	T	H	U	R	U
C	H	O	C	O	L	A	T	E	K
A	A	P	W	L	R	S	K	I	K
N	N	S	P	I	N	A	N	D	A
D	D	I	L	D	N	W	H	E	H
L	L	P	L	A	M	G	X	L	Z
E	C	L	A	Y	G	I	F	T	S

Hanukkah	menorah	candle	light
glowing	window	dreidel	clay
spin	play	chocolate	gifts
holiday			

2. On a separate sheet of paper, draw a menorah with candles lit.

Christmas

Christmas means "Christ's birth." Many songs have been written about Jesus' birth. This story is sometimes called the Nativity, which also means "the birth." In the blanks below, fill in the missing people, places, and things to complete the Christmas story.

The Nativity

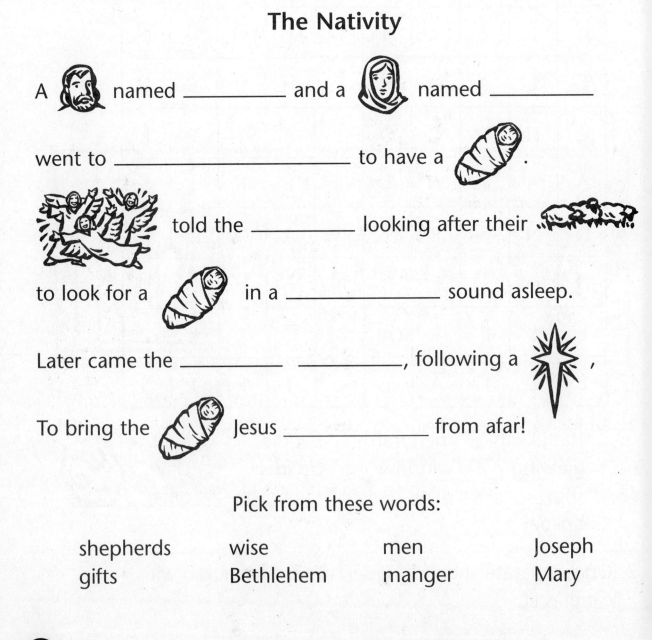

A [face] named _____ and a [face] named _____

went to _____ to have a [baby] .

[angels] told the _____ looking after their [sheep]

to look for a [baby] in a _____ sound asleep.

Later came the _____ _____, following a [star] ,

To bring the [baby] Jesus _____ from afar!

Pick from these words:

shepherds	wise	men	Joseph
gifts	Bethlehem	manger	Mary

Name _____ Date _____

Presidents' Day

Presidents' Day in February celebrates the birthdays of two presidents, George Washington and Abraham Lincoln.

Abraham Lincoln was born in a log cabin in Kentucky in 1809. He was President during the Civil War. Because Lincoln's side won the war, all of the United States stayed together as one country. Lincoln signed the law that ended slavery. You can visit the Lincoln Memorial in Washington, D.C.

1. Where have you seen President Lincoln? Color in these famous Lincoln symbols.

2. If you could meet George Washington or Abraham Lincoln, which one would you want to meet? Why? Explain your choice on the lines below.

_____

_____

Purim

Listen to this story of brave Queen Esther. When your teacher says the words for the pictures, you say the phrase, do the action, and make the sound listed for that picture.

 The King: "Your Majesty." Boys bow. (*do-so* fanfare on xylophone)

Mordechai: "Aha!" Point finger up. (triangle)

 Party: "Hurray!" Shouts, whoops, and cheers. (clapping)

Jews: "Shalom." Clasp hands to heart. (tambourine)

Esther: "Ooo! Ahh!" Girls curtsy. (finger cymbals)

Haman: "Boo! Hiss!" Shake fist above head. (loud racket)

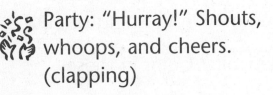   

loved a ... . He also loved a girl named ... and her

cousin ... , his loyal servant. ... had a ... and made ...

his queen. ... and ... were ... , but no one knew ...

was a ... , not even ... . had another servant named

... . hated ... . asked ... for all the ... to be

Purim (continued)

killed, and 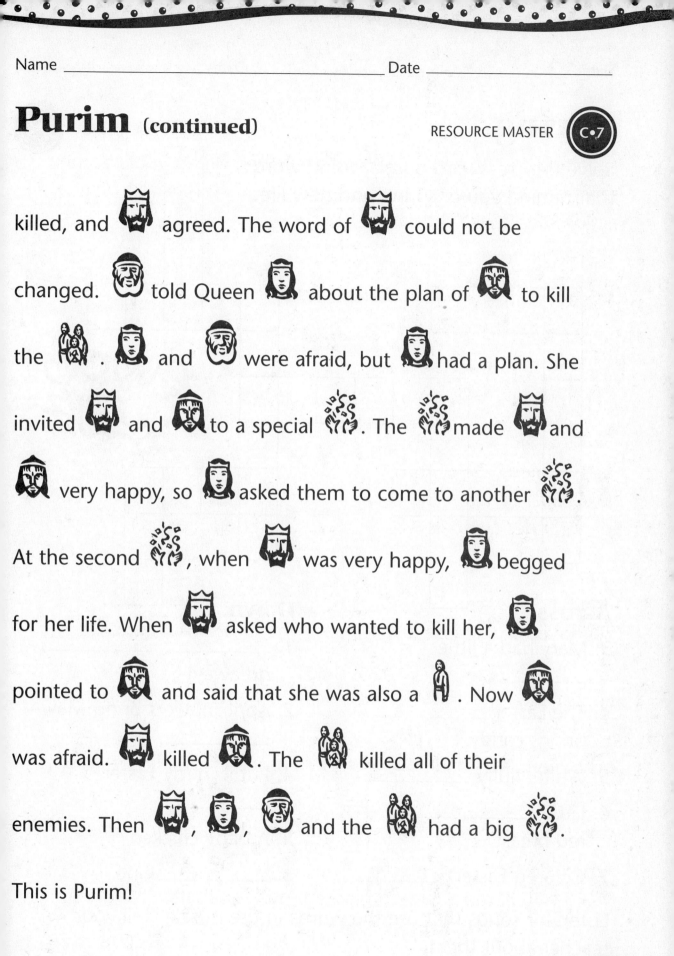 agreed. The word of could not be

changed. told Queen about the plan of to kill

the . and were afraid, but had a plan. She

invited and to a special . The made and

very happy, so asked them to come to another .

At the second , when was very happy, begged

for her life. When asked who wanted to kill her,

pointed to and said that she was also a . Now

was afraid. killed . The killed all of their

enemies. Then , , and the had a big .

This is Purim!

Name _____ Date _____

Spring

Solve the crossword puzzle, using words that remind you of spring and new life.

Across

3. Mary had a little _____.

4. The Easter _____ brings candy.

5. White, fluffy _____

6. Little _____ red breast

7. Colored Easter _____

Down

1. _____, _____, go away!

2. April showers bring May _____.

4. Put it in my Easter _____.

5. A baby chicken

8. _____shine

Listen for songs that use the words in the puzzle. Tell your teacher about them.

Name _____ Date _____

Cinco de Mayo

Read about the instruments in a mariachi band. Draw a line between the name and the picture of each instrument.

1. trumpet
A brass instrument used in
marching bands and orchestras

a.

2. violin
A small stringed instrument held
under the chin and played with a bow

b.

3. vihuela
A round-backed stringed instrument
played like a guitar or mandolin

c.

4. guitar
A five-stringed instrument
used in folk and other popular music

d.

5. guitarrón
A extra-large guitar that has a low
bass sound

e.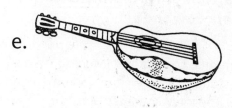

Listening Map Instructions

LM-3 Ballet Music from *Iphigénie en Aulide* by Christoph Gluck

Use with Unit 1, Lesson 5

Distribute a copy of the listening map to each student. Direct them to look at the map and see how it is broken up into different sections. The first part is the Introduction, the second section is labeled A, the third section is labeled B, and the last part is called the Coda. The Introduction is unlike the rest of the piece. There are strong chords or "beats" that are interspersed with softer "busy" elements. Tell students that the bursts in the introduction are these loud chords.

Section A follows a very specific rhythmic pattern of strong and weak beats, indicated by the large and small symbols. The large symbol is a strong beat and the small symbol is the weaker beat. The instruments at the side show the main instruments that the student will hear in different parts of the A section.

Section B is very flowing and doesn't have the strong rhythmic pattern of section A. The squiggly lines indicate the movement of the music in this section. Point out the repeat symbols and how the music goes back and starts over.

The Coda begins like the third line of section A, but it ends in a number of strong chords.

LM-6 Akinla from *African Suite* by Fela Sowande

Use with Unit 3, Lesson 3

Distribute a copy of the listening map to each student. There is only one theme in this piece. The interest comes from the differences in scoring, or assigning instruments. There are also changes in methods of playing (loud/soft, bowed/pizzicato, connected notes/staccato, etc.). The style changes from one section to another, even though the theme stays the same. The different "variations" of texture are not all of equal lengths, so this is not a map to use for counting beats, only as a way of recognizing changes from one style to another.

Students should first hear the theme (it varies somewhat as the piece goes on, but the rhythm and contour stay quite consistent). Play the melodic theme shown at the top on piano, xylophone, or any pitched instrument, and tell the students to listen for this theme in every section. Have students listen once to the piece without the map, raising their hands when they think the style or texture changes. Ask them to acknowledge only the big changes. Remind them that not all the sections are the same length, so they must listen for big changes in the texture.

Using the map, have the students indicate each style change by tracing their fingers down to each new design.

Here is a description of the sections, with timings:

Introduction: (jumps around and overlaps on the theme, high and low) 0:00

1. Middle strings in unison 0:22
2. Busy string figures against the theme 0:50
3. Violins playing the theme 1:19
4. Violas with shimmery violin background 1:38
5. Cellos with pizzicato accompaniment and agitated background 1:54
6. All high strings together 2:18
7. All high strings with busy bass 2:33

Coda Arch of low strings to high and back to low 2:50

Listening Map Instructions

LM-7 Symphonic Dances Op. 64, No. 4 (excerpt) by Edvard Grieg

Use with Unit 3, Lesson 5

Distribute a copy of the listening map to each student. In this map, as in the musical selection, there are landmarks. Have the students listen for these landmarks as they follow the climber up one side of the mountain and down the other. Have them notice the changes in mood, the upward surge as the brass and strings "help" the climber reach the top. Have them listen for the stormy brass on the downward climb, and the accelerando as the climber nears home.

Timings:
Start: 00 Horn at :02
Strings at 00:16 ("Waterfalls" strings with low brass at 00:30)
Woodwinds at 00:58
Brass at 1:04
Strings at 1:12 and last part of the climb at 1:22
Strings at summit at 1:26
Horns and Trombones (storm) at 1:48
Strong brass and starting down at 2:36
Accelerando and home from 3:08 to the end.

LM-8 Concerto for Violin and Oboe BWV 1060, Adagio (excerpt) by Johann Sebastian Bach

Use with Unit 4, Lesson 1

Distribute a copy of the listening map to each student. Relate this musical "conversation" to the lesson on pupil pages 126 and 127. In this piece the oboe and violin take turns "speaking," but sometimes talk on top of one another. They are accompanied by a low cello part that holds everything together, and with pizzicato strings that punctuate each measure.

Have the students listen once and discuss which solo instrument has the most to say (they are pretty equal, but the oboe, because of the long first phrase, may have the upper hand). Project the map so that all students can see. Play the piece again, and have them listen once as you point to each pizzicato graphic on beats 2 and 3. (The students do not need to know the meter or which beats are playing. It is an easy rhythm to "feel.")

Listen with the map, tapping each of the pizzicato starbursts to follow the musical conversation, noting the times when the two instruments play alone, when they play together, and when they seem to be answering one another.

LM-10 Effie Goes Folk Dancing by Alec Wilder

Use with Unit 5, Lesson 1

Distribute a copy of the listening map to each student. This listening map is easy to follow. Effie dancing (represented by the tuba) is in seven sections, and there are piano interludes, some very short, some longer. Discuss the story line with students before you listen.

Top panel:

Effie peeks out from a stage curtain, the pianist plays, Effie dances, pianist plays.

Second panel (starts at 00:26):

Effie dances in a slightly different pose, Pianist. Effie dances again—new pose.

Third panel (starts at 00:50)

Effie dances with more abandon. Pianist. Effie dances. (music is the same as #1.)

Fourth panel (starts at 1:40)

Effie bows. Effie runs offstage and tail is all we see as she disappears behind stage curtain.

Students should note the tempo changes, the ritards at the ends of most "dance" sections, and the accelerando at the end as Effie runs offstage.

Listening Map Instructions

LM-13 Young Person's Guide to the Orchestra (excerpt) by Benjamin Britten

Use with Unit 6, Lesson 6

Distribute a copy of the listening map to each student. Each section of this statement of the theme is played by different sections of the orchestra (the full orchestra plays first and last). Have students note that the conductor has climbed the podium via three steps (these are leaps of a third in the music.) Remind students what a leap is and play several leaps of thirds in a D minor chord (d f a.) The opening notes of the theme are an upward motion that sound like climbing steps, and can be used as a landmark for each section. Have students identify the instrument families and any instruments they know before they listen.

Timings:
Theme: at 00:00
Woodwinds: 0:42
Brass: 1:11
Strings: 1:42
Percussion: 2:07
Tutti: 2:26

LM-16 The Washington Post by John Philip Sousa

Use with SPOTLIGHT ON CELEBRATIONS

Distribute a copy of the listening map to each student. As they listen to the music help them identify the different leading instruments in each section. The map depicts the image of a parade, often the venue for John Phillip Sousa's marches. In the introduction, the trumpet is heard over all the other instruments. Following the parade into the A float, students will hear a concert band with full instrumentation. The melody is carried by the trumpets, flutes, and trombones, with drums and cymbals playing in the background. Moving on to the B float, the trombone is heard playing a countermelody, with notes rising over the other instruments. On the C float, the woodwinds take over the melody followed by a musical interlude with mostly trombone and flute/piccolo answering each other, followed by the sound of the cymbals. On the second C float, the trombones can be heard with an equally prominent countermelody to the other instruments.

Sousa is known as "The March King" because his marches were such an integral part of American life in his day. He wrote marches for all manner of occasions. One example is the well known Washington Post march. This piece was not written in honor of the Marine barracks (the Marine "post," as it were) in Washington as one might imply from its title (and realizing Sousa's strong ties to that place); it was written instead for the newspaper The Washington Post to promote an essay contest sponsored by that newspaper.

LM-17 In the Hall of the Mountain King from Peer Gynt Suite No. 1, Op. 46 by Edvard Grieg

Use with SPOTLIGHT ON CELEBRATIONS

Distribute a copy of the listening map to each child. Echo-clap the rhythm of the theme that is at the top of the map, first in 2-measure units, then all together. Have children clap the rhythm at slow and fast tempos. Have the children look at the map before listening and ask them what they notice about the way the boy is moving along the path. (He starts out slowly and goes faster and faster.) Ask the children what they notice about the path. (It is narrow at the top and wider at the bottom, like a crescendo marking, meaning "to get louder.") Notice the numbers. Each number stands for one occurrence of the theme. Number 19 is the coda, the fastest part of the selection. The troll at the bottom is the Mountain King.

Ballet Music
from *Iphigénie en Aulide*

Introduction

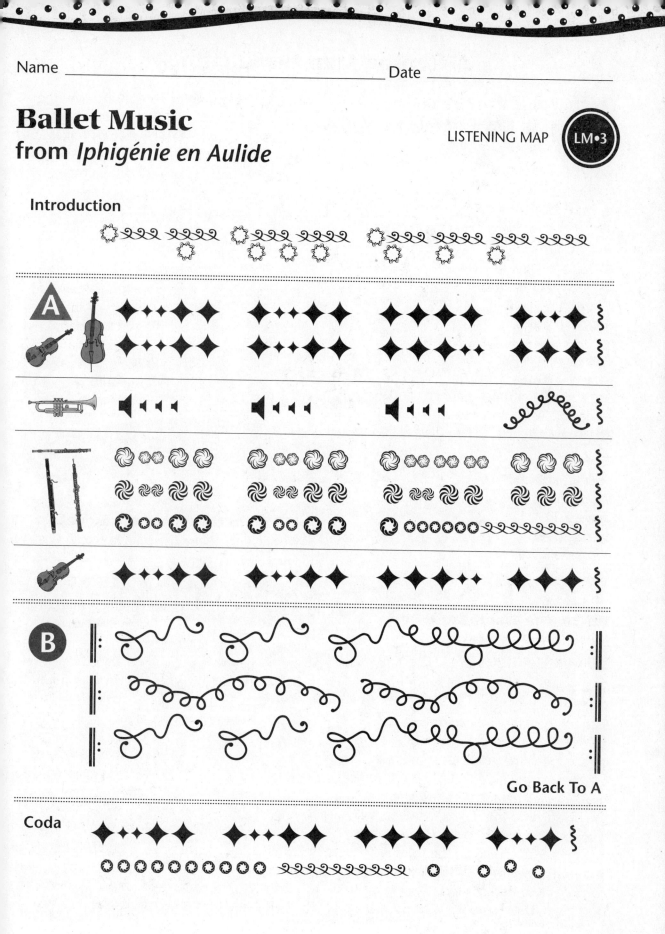

Go Back To A

Coda

Akinla from *African Suite*

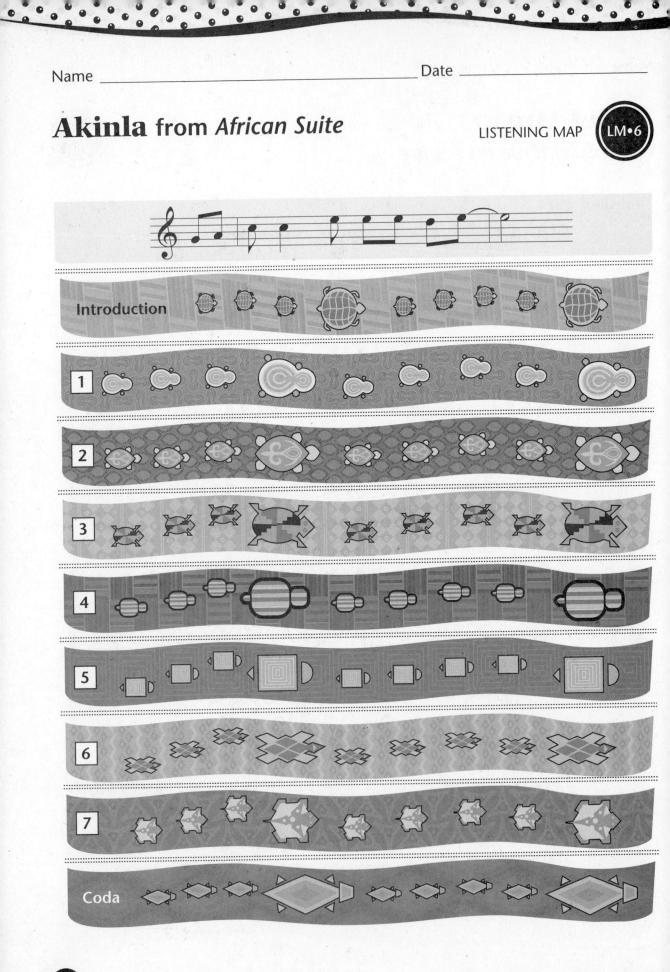

Introduction

1

2

3

4

5

6

7

Coda

Symphonic Dances Op. 64, No. 4 (excerpt)

LISTENING MAP LM•7

Concerto for Violin and Oboe BWV 1060, Adagio (excerpt)

LISTENING MAP LM•8

A Conversation:

USE WITH GRADE 2, UNIT 4, LESSON 1

Effie Goes Folk Dancing

LISTENING MAP **LM•10**

Young Person's Guide to the Orchestra (excerpt)

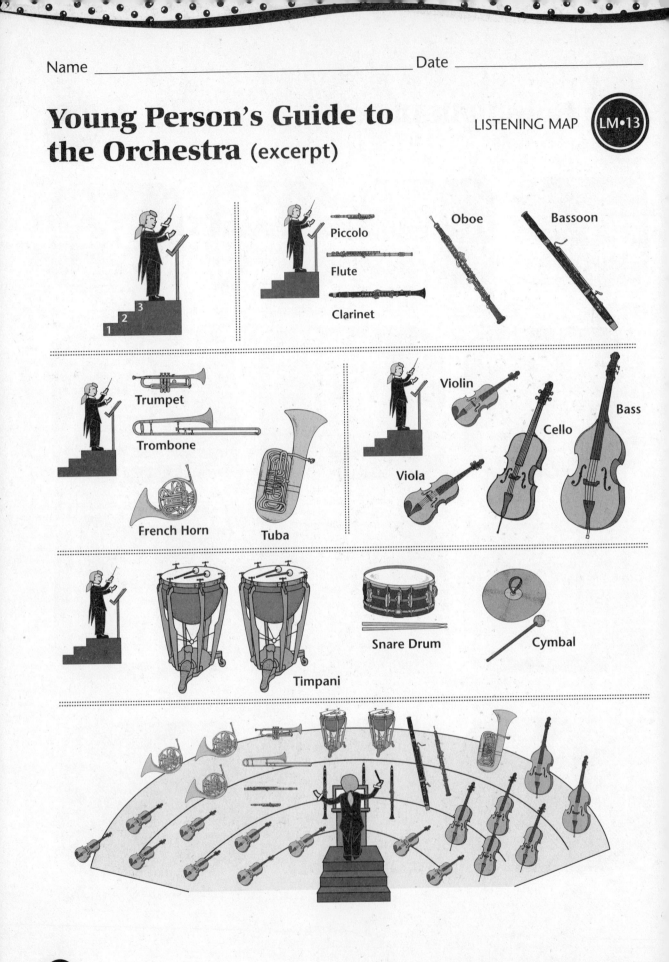

Piccolo

Flute

Clarinet

Oboe

Bassoon

3
2
1

Trumpet

Trombone

French Horn

Tuba

Violin

Viola

Cello

Bass

Timpani

Snare Drum

Cymbal

USE WITH GRADE 2, UNIT 6, LESSON 6

The Washington Post

INTRODUCTION

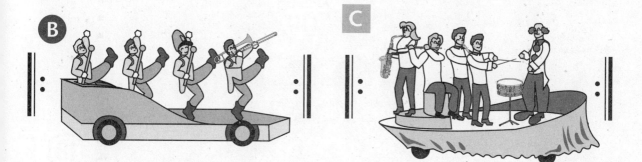

INTERLUDE

Go back to the Interlude to the end

In the Hall of the Mountain King

from *Peer Gynt Suite No. 1, Op. 46*

Introduction to Signed Songs

by The Reverend Dr. Peggy A. Johnson, pastor
Christ United Methodist Church of the Deaf

The use of sign language along with vocal music has become a popular way of adding interest and expression to a song. Frequently a student who struggles with vocal music will find a successful outlet for expression through the use of sign language. Sign language has been used as an educational tool for reading comprehension and language development. Typically it appears as a picture for every spoken or written English word. This is known as "Signed English." It follows the grammar of English.

American Sign Language (ASL) is different from Signed English. It uses signs for words or concepts, but the grammar is produced with the eyes and face and through the movements of the body. It does not follow the word order of spoken English for the most part and has its own structure. ASL is the native language of people who describe themselves as Culturally Deaf. Deaf Culture is a community of people consisting of deaf and hard-of-hearing people who:

• use ASL,

• have primary personal relationships with people who also use this language,

• have typically attended state residential schools for the deaf where ASL is the mode of communication and instruction, and

• have unique history, traditions, and advocacy organizations.

For people in the Deaf Culture, ASL is used in their music and poetry, not Signed English.

It is difficult for a hearing person to sing an English word-order song and to sign in ASL at the same time. Most of the sign language section of this book is done in English word-order for that reason. However, some ASL grammar is incorporated for the purpose of linguistical awareness, and ASL grammar often creates a more artistic rendering of the movements. A phrase such as "lift up your eyes" in English would be best translated into ASL as "your eyes, lift up." The latter is more effective in a signed song because ending on a sign such as "lift up" has a better flow.

Hearing people who are fascinated by and attracted to signed music might consider taking a course on ASL. It would help increase one's skill in the language. People who study "foreign" languages often develop a sensitivity for the culture and people from which the language sprang. It is a sign of respect for the culture of the people for whom this language is their native language.

A good music program provides many benefits to students and teachers. Multicultural awareness is increased when we sing songs in Spanish or German or Japanese. By "singing" in ASL, students can gain multicultural awareness of the Deaf Culture.

Rules for Signed Singing

1) Every word does not need to be signed. Keep the signs flowing one to the other and be sensitive to the length of the word in the music. The sign for a whole-note word should be stretched out longer and slower than a quarter-note word.

2) Right-handed and left-handed people sign opposite because there is a dominant, active hand and a passive hand in many signs. For a performance, it is best to have everyone signing one way or the other, either everyone do it right-handed or everyone do it left-handed.

3) When teaching a song, it is ideal to teach it with your back to the students facing a large mirror. In that way the directionality is correct. When a teacher faces a group of students and signs, the students tend to mirror the teacher, and then the sign goes in the opposite direction.

4) A person's face needs to be appropriate to the mood of the word being sung. "Sad" should look sad, "joyful" should look joyful, etc.

5) If at all possible, invite a native signer to assist with the teaching of the song. This shows respect for the Deaf Culture, and a live example of a sign is always preferable to a drawn picture of a sign in a book.

Perfection is not the goal. The joy of music expressed in sign language can occur even when the signs are not performed perfectly.

Alphabet and Numbers

SIGNING MASTER **S•1**

MANUAL ALPHABET AND NUMBERS 1–10

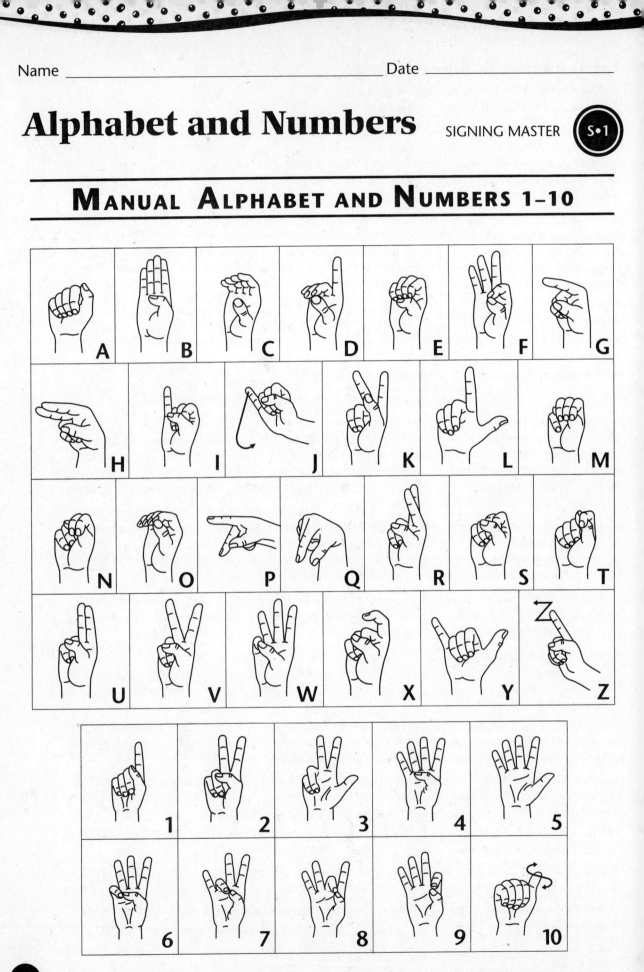

USE WITH GRADE 2, SIGNING

You Are My Sunshine (Page 1)

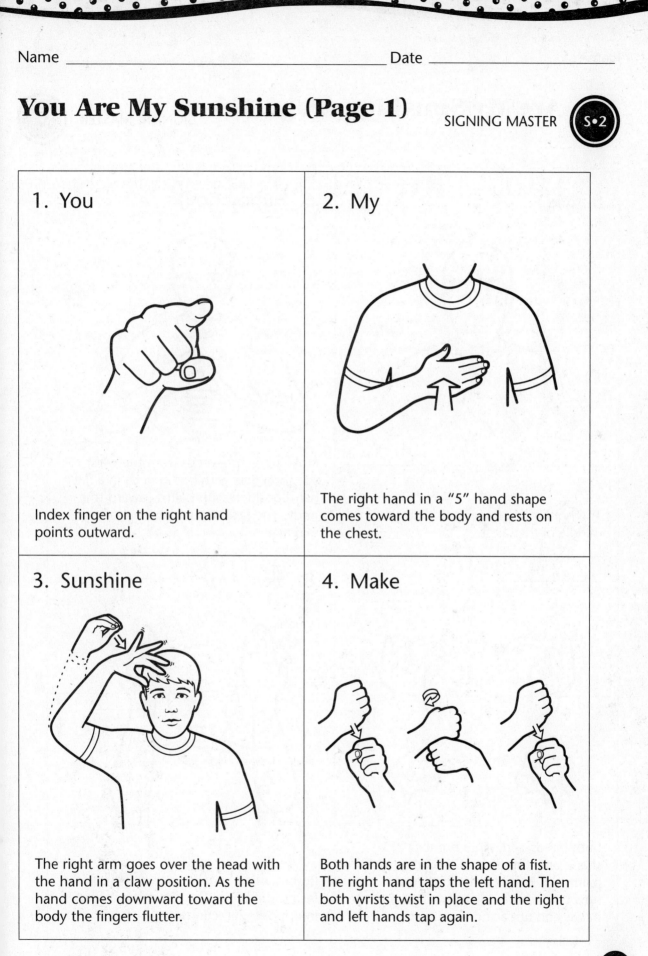

1. You

Index finger on the right hand points outward.

2. My

The right hand in a "5" hand shape comes toward the body and rests on the chest.

3. Sunshine

The right arm goes over the head with the hand in a claw position. As the hand comes downward toward the body the fingers flutter.

4. Make

Both hands are in the shape of a fist. The right hand taps the left hand. Then both wrists twist in place and the right and left hands tap again.

You Are My Sunshine (Page 2)

SIGNING MASTER **S•2**

5. Me

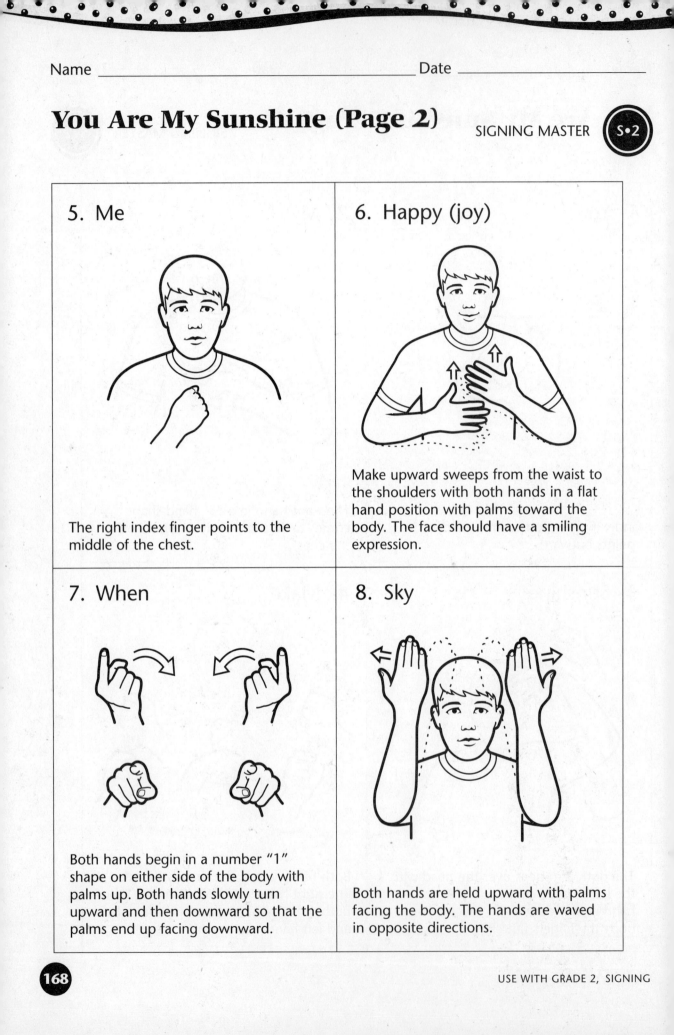

The right index finger points to the middle of the chest.

6. Happy (joy)

Make upward sweeps from the waist to the shoulders with both hands in a flat hand position with palms toward the body. The face should have a smiling expression.

7. When

Both hands begin in a number "1" shape on either side of the body with palms up. Both hands slowly turn upward and then downward so that the palms end up facing downward.

8. Sky

Both hands are held upward with palms facing the body. The hands are waved in opposite directions.

You Are My Sunshine (Page 3)

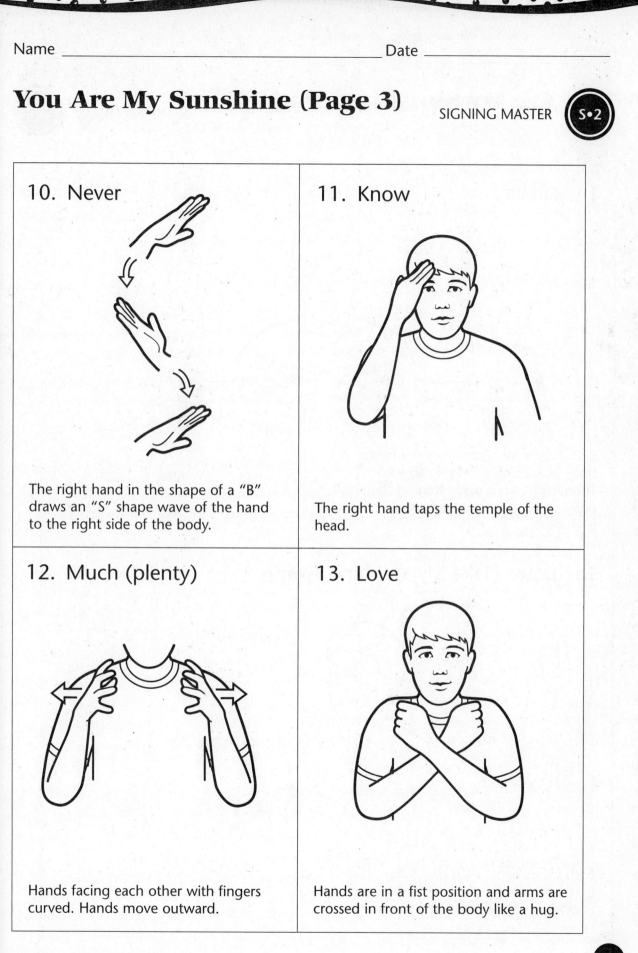

10. Never

The right hand in the shape of a "B" draws an "S" shape wave of the hand to the right side of the body.

11. Know

The right hand taps the temple of the head.

12. Much (plenty)

Hands facing each other with fingers curved. Hands move outward.

13. Love

Hands are in a fist position and arms are crossed in front of the body like a hug.

You Are My Sunshine (Page 4)

14. Don't

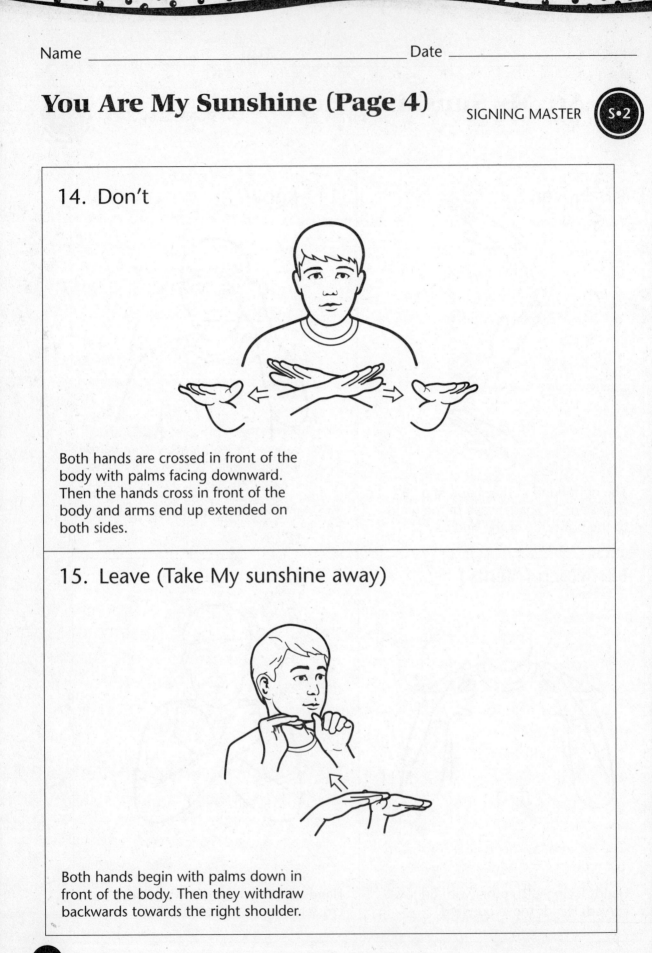

Both hands are crossed in front of the body with palms facing downward. Then the hands cross in front of the body and arms end up extended on both sides.

15. Leave (Take My sunshine away)

Both hands begin with palms down in front of the body. Then they withdraw backwards towards the right shoulder.

I Saw Three Ships

SIGNING MASTER S•3

1. Christmas

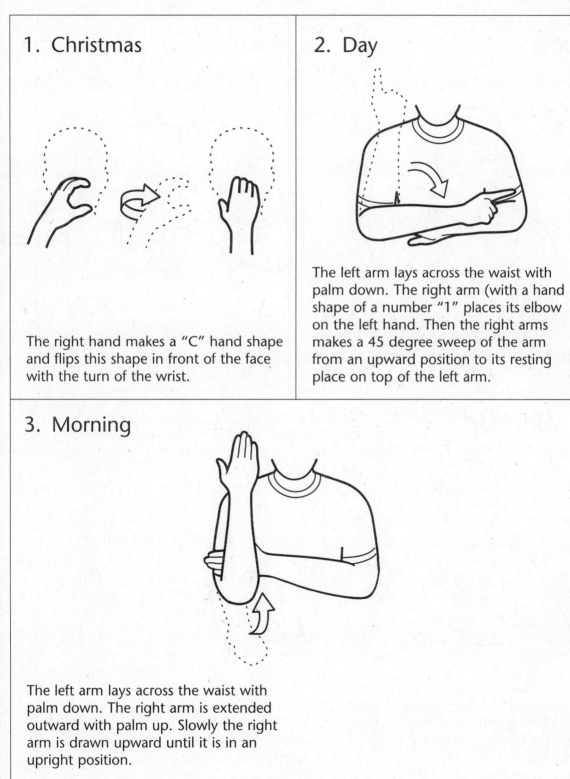

The right hand makes a "C" hand shape and flips this shape in front of the face with the turn of the wrist.

2. Day

The left arm lays across the waist with palm down. The right arm (with a hand shape of a number "1" places its elbow on the left hand. Then the right arms makes a 45 degree sweep of the arm from an upward position to its resting place on top of the left arm.

3. Morning

The left arm lays across the waist with palm down. The right arm is extended outward with palm up. Slowly the right arm is drawn upward until it is in an upright position.

We Wish You a Merry Christmas (Page 1)

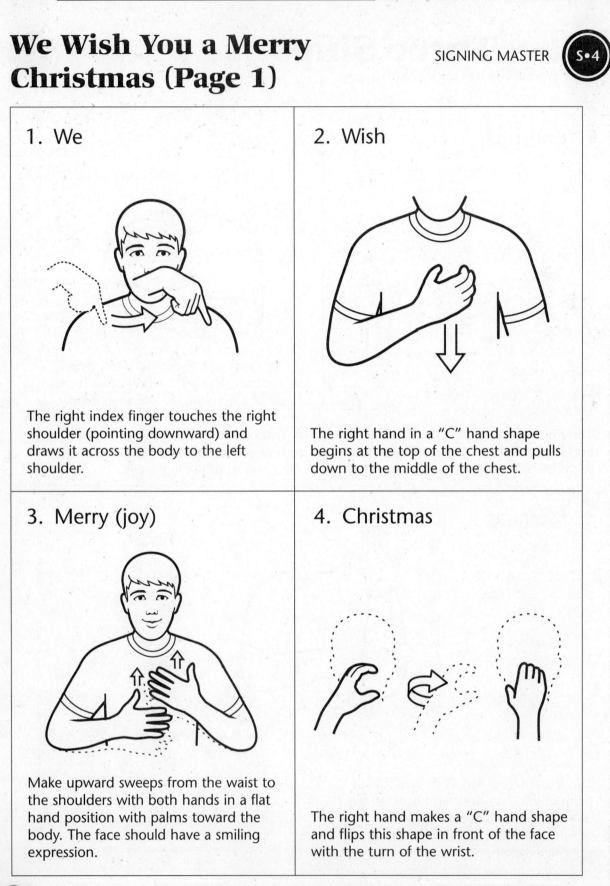

1. We

The right index finger touches the right shoulder (pointing downward) and draws it across the body to the left shoulder.

2. Wish

The right hand in a "C" hand shape begins at the top of the chest and pulls down to the middle of the chest.

3. Merry (joy)

Make upward sweeps from the waist to the shoulders with both hands in a flat hand position with palms toward the body. The face should have a smiling expression.

4. Christmas

The right hand makes a "C" hand shape and flips this shape in front of the face with the turn of the wrist.

We Wish You a Merry Christmas (Page 2)

5. New

The left hand is in front of the body with palms up and slightly curved. The right hand with palms up and slightly curved brushes the palm of the left hand with the back of the hand in an upward motion.

6. Year

Both hands are in the shape of a fist and they make circles around each other in front of the body.

You'll Sing a Song and I'll Sing a Song (Page 1)

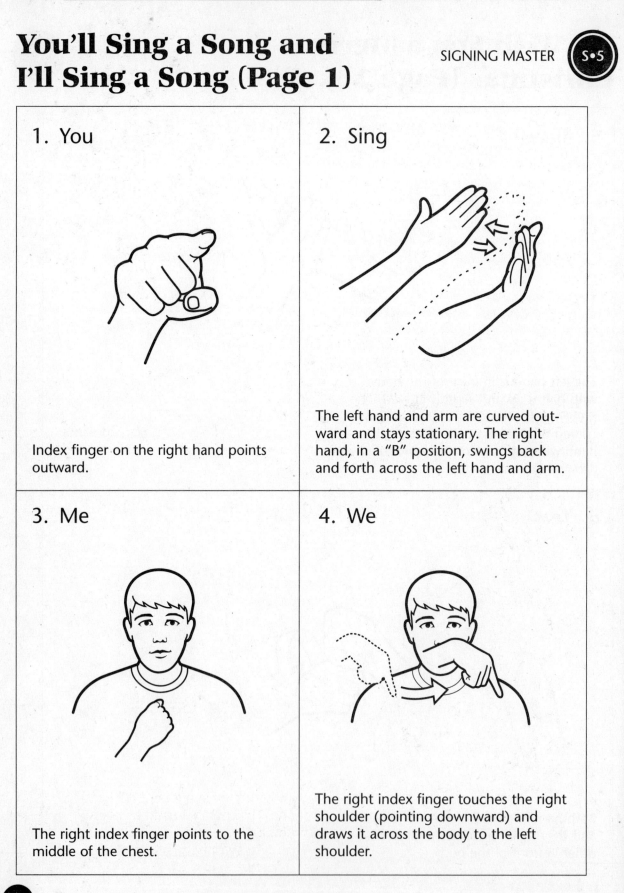

1. You

Index finger on the right hand points outward.

2. Sing

The left hand and arm are curved outward and stays stationary. The right hand, in a "B" position, swings back and forth across the left hand and arm.

3. Me

The right index finger points to the middle of the chest.

4. We

The right index finger touches the right shoulder (pointing downward) and draws it across the body to the left shoulder.

You'll Sing a Song and I'll Sing a Song (Page 2)

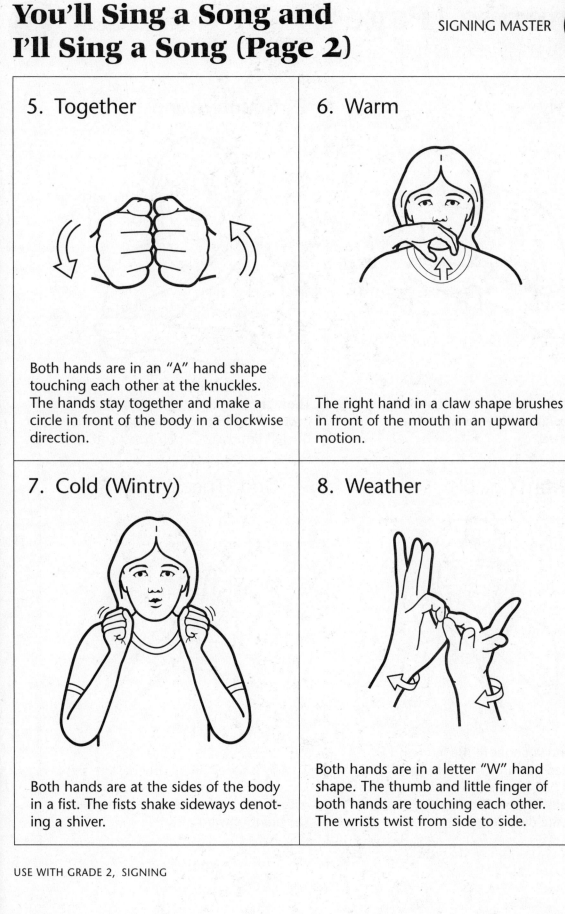

5. Together

Both hands are in an "A" hand shape touching each other at the knuckles. The hands stay together and make a circle in front of the body in a clockwise direction.

6. Warm

The right hand in a claw shape brushes in front of the mouth in an upward motion.

7. Cold (Wintry)

Both hands are at the sides of the body in a fist. The fists shake sideways denoting a shiver.

8. Weather

Both hands are in a letter "W" hand shape. The thumb and little finger of both hands are touching each other. The wrists twist from side to side.

America (Page 1)

SIGNING MASTER **S•6**

1. My

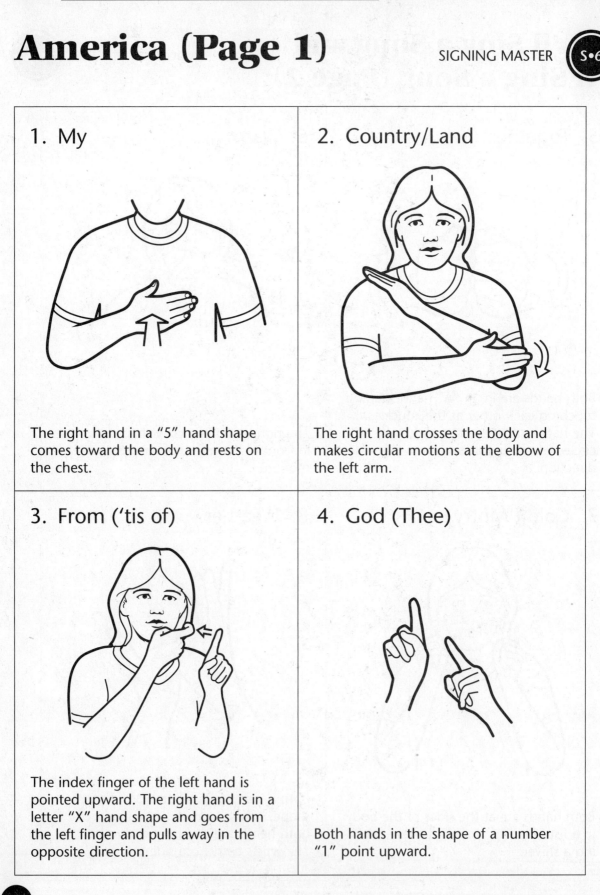

The right hand in a "5" hand shape comes toward the body and rests on the chest.

2. Country/Land

The right hand crosses the body and makes circular motions at the elbow of the left arm.

3. From ('tis of)

The index finger of the left hand is pointed upward. The right hand is in a letter "X" hand shape and goes from the left finger and pulls away in the opposite direction.

4. God (Thee)

Both hands in the shape of a number "1" point upward.

USE WITH GRADE 2, SIGNING

America (Page 2)

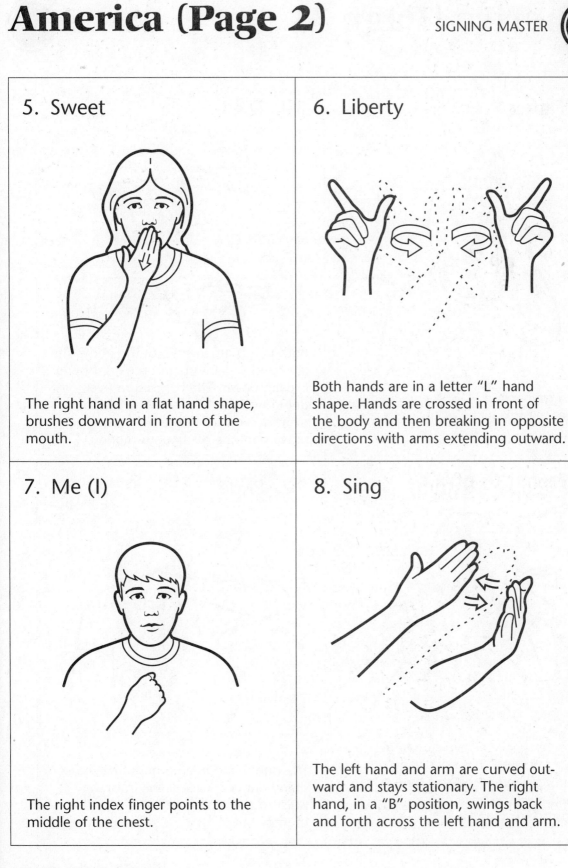

5. Sweet

The right hand in a flat hand shape, brushes downward in front of the mouth.

6. Liberty

Both hands are in a letter "L" hand shape. Hands are crossed in front of the body and then breaking in opposite directions with arms extending outward.

7. Me (I)

The right index finger points to the middle of the chest.

8. Sing

The left hand and arm are curved outward and stays stationary. The right hand, in a "B" position, swings back and forth across the left hand and arm.

America (Page 3)

9. Father

Right hand in "5" hand shape with thumb touching forehead.

10. Died

Both hands are in front of the body. The left hand is palm up and the right hand is palm down. The hands turn over going from left to right. The left palm turns downward as the right palm turns upward in one continuous motion.

11. People (Pilgrim)

Both hands are in a "P" hand shape in front of the body making little circles in opposite directions.

12. Pride

The right hand in a number "10" hand shape draws a vertical line from the waist to the top of the chest with the thumb.

America (Page 4)

13. From

The index finger of the left hand is pointed upward. The right hand is in a letter "X" hand shape and goes from the left finger and pulls away in the opposite direction.

14. Every

Both hands are in a number "10" hand shape. The right hand brushes sideways and downward next to the left hand.

15. Mountain (mountainside)

Both hands are in a letter "A" hand shape to the side of the body with the right hand on top of the left. Then both hands open to a "B" hand shape and glide upward and to the right.

16. Let

Both hands are at the sides with palms facing inward. They both point the fingertip side of the hand in and upward direction with two quick motions.

America (Page 5)

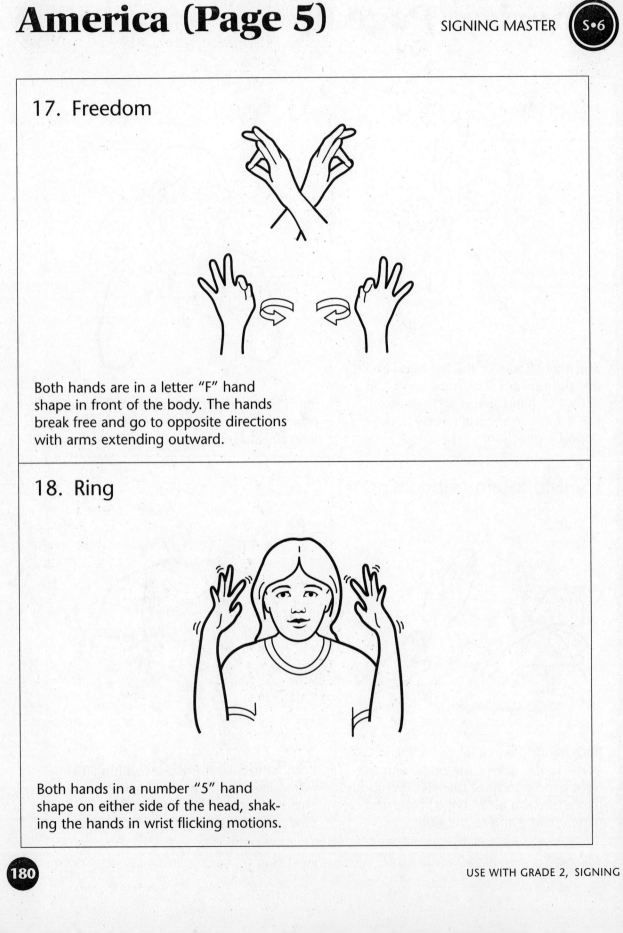

17. Freedom

Both hands are in a letter "F" hand shape in front of the body. The hands break free and go to opposite directions with arms extending outward.

18. Ring

Both hands in a number "5" hand shape on either side of the head, shaking the hands in wrist flicking motions.

This is My Country (Page 1)

1. This

Both hands are in a number "1" hand shape in front of the body with the finger pointing downward two times.

2. My

The right hand in a "5" hand shape comes toward the body and rests on the chest.

3. Country

The right hand crosses the body and makes circular motions at the elbow of the left arm.

4. Birth

The left hand holds the right hand in a right angle position in front of the body. Both hands then move away from the body maintaining the holding position.

This is My Country (Page 2)

5. Choice

The left hand is in front of the body in a shape of a letter "V". The palm is toward the body. The right hand approaches the left hand and in a letter "F" hand shape as if picking something off of it and draws it away.

6. Best (Grandest)

The right hand in a flat position with palm facing inward sweeps across the mouth and moves to the shape of a number "10" at the side of the head above the ear.

7. Earth

The left hand is in the shape of a fist with palm facing down. The right hand thumb and forefinger grips the left hand fist and wiggles it back and forth.

8. Hear

The right hand in a letter "C" hand shape holds it up to the right ear.

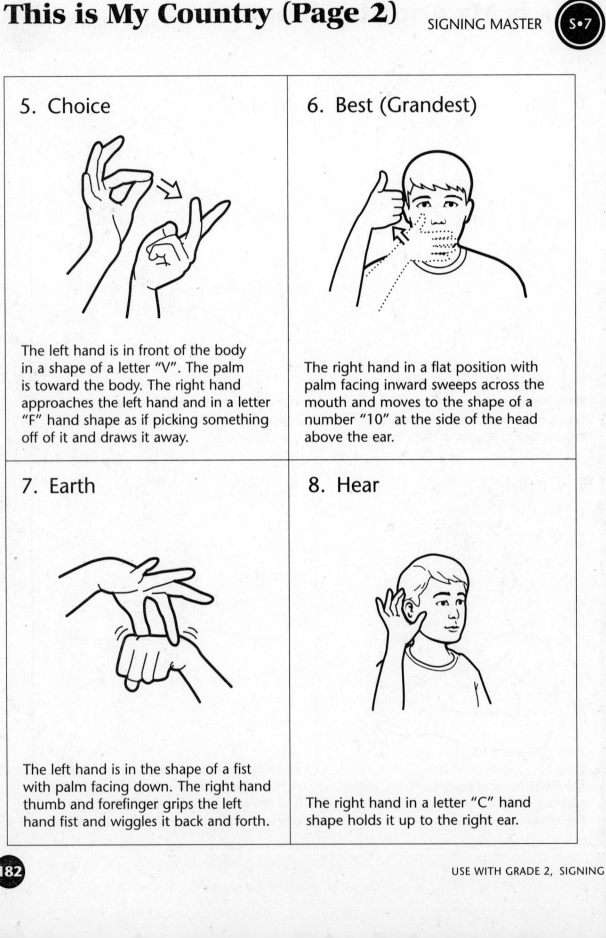

This is My Country (Page 3)

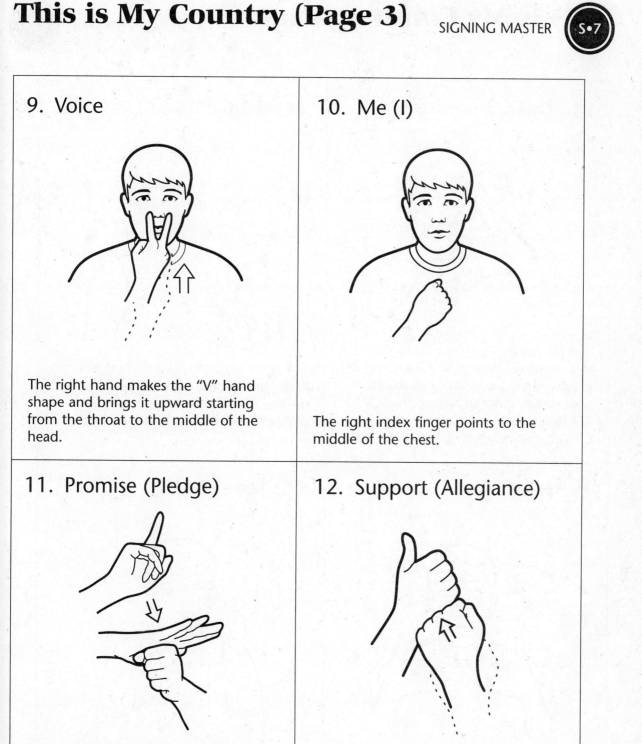

9. Voice

The right hand makes the "V" hand shape and brings it upward starting from the throat to the middle of the head.

10. Me (I)

The right index finger points to the middle of the chest.

11. Promise (Pledge)

The right hand touches the lips and then brings the hand down to the left hand which is in the shape of a fist. The right hand becomes flat and taps the top of the fist.

12. Support (Allegiance)

Both hands are in a number "10" hand shape. The left fist is under the right fist. The left fist taps the right fist from below.

This is My Country (Page 4)

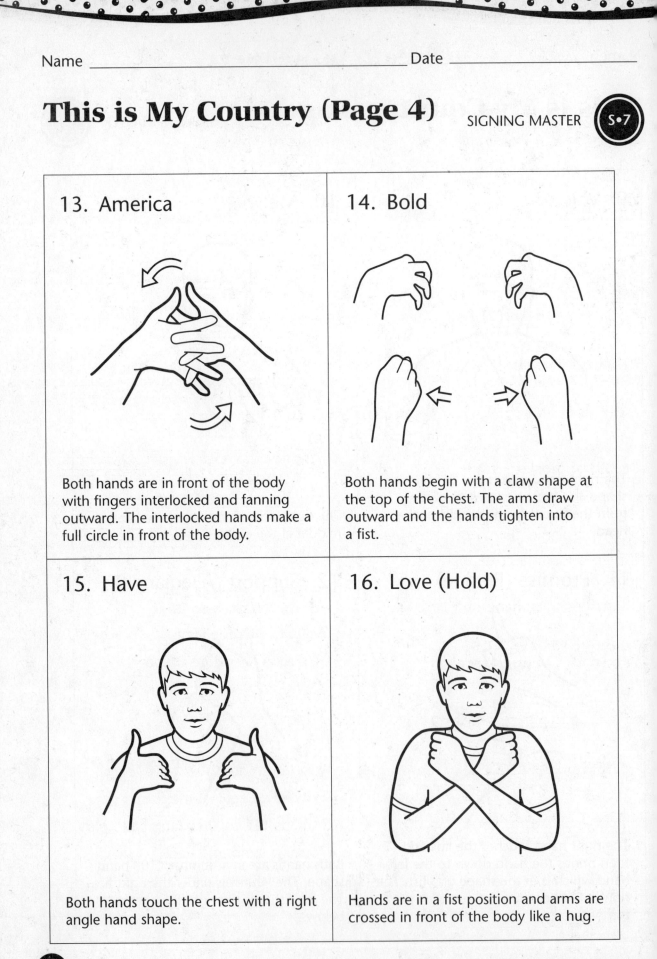

13. America

Both hands are in front of the body with fingers interlocked and fanning outward. The interlocked hands make a full circle in front of the body.

14. Bold

Both hands begin with a claw shape at the top of the chest. The arms draw outward and the hands tighten into a fist.

15. Have

Both hands touch the chest with a right angle hand shape.

16. Love (Hold)

Hands are in a fist position and arms are crossed in front of the body like a hug.

Grade 2 Answer Key

Resource Master 1–6
Rhythm for a Poem

Sun - flow-er, dai - sy,

Lil - y, tu - lip, rose,

I - ris, li - lacs, glad - i - o - las,

Flow - er gar - den grows!

Resource Master 1–8
Mid-Unit Review

1. d 2. e 3. a 4. c 5. b
6. h 7. j 8. i 9. f 10. g

Resource Master 1–9
Rhythm Instruments

Woods: rhythm sticks, wood blocks

Metals: triangle, gong

Shakers and Rattles: tambourine, jingle bells

Drums: bongos, hand drum

Resource Master 1–10
So and *Mi* Change Places

1.

2.

3.

Resource Master 2–4
Sets of Two

Resource Master 2–5
Finding *La*

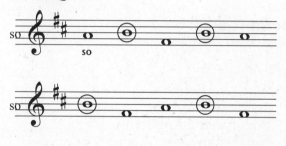

Resource Master 2–6
Circle the Strong Beat

Mary had a little lamb,
Its fleece was white as snow,
And everywhere that Mary went,
The lamb was sure to go.

It followed her to school one day,
Which was against the rule:
It made the children laugh and play
To see a lamb at school.

Grade 2 Answer Key

Resource Master 2–7
Mi, *So*, and *La*

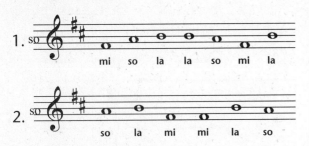

3. Answers will vary. Make sure students have followed the guidelines.

Resource Master 2–8
Mid-Unit Review

1.

2. Possible answers: S w w, S w w, S w w; w w S, w w S, w w S; or w S w, w S w, w S w.

Resource Master 2–10
The Brass Band

1. e 2. d 3. b 4. c 5. a

Resource Master 3–4 Half Notes

Resource Master 3–5 *Do*, *Mi*, and *So*

3. Answers will vary. Make sure that students have followed the guidelines.

Resource Master 3–6
Strings Make Music

1. The violin, the viola, the cello, and the double bass have **four** strings.

2. You play these instruments with a **bow**.

3. You can also pluck the strings with your **fingers**.

4. The biggest string instrument is the **double bass**.

186

Grade 2 Answer Key

Resource Master 3–8
Mid-Unit Review

A is for South **Africa.**

B is for **Brazil.**

C is for **cello.**

D is for *do.*

E is for **expressive.**

F is for **fanfare.**

G is for **guzheng.**

H is for **half note.**

Resource Master 3–10
Strings Make Music

4.

5.

Resource Master 3–11
Music Around the World

Possible answers by continent:

North America

Composers/Musicians: Robert Dickow, Leontyne Price, the American Horn Quartet

Songs/Music: "This Is My Country," "Land of the Silver Birch," "Entrance Fanfare," "He's Got the Whole World in His Hands"

South America

Musicians: Caribbean Steel Band, Carmen Miranda

Songs/Music: "Shake the Papaya Down," "Mama Paquita," "Mama eu quero," Brazilian Carnival song, "Procession at Pisac," "En Nuestra Tierra" (On Our Beautiful Planet Earth)

Instruments: Bolivian sheep horn, Peruvian conch shell horn

Africa

Songs/Music: "Pata, Pata," "Sorida," "Akinla" from African Suite

Musicians: Miriam Makeba, Chief Fela Sowande

Instruments: mbira, African shakers

Asia

Songs/Music: "Tal Tta Ro Ka Cha" (Come, Pick the Moon), "Evening Party," "Hik Besenda Gurau"

Composers: Tae-Hyun Park, He Luting

Instruments: guzheng, erhu, yunluo

Europe

Songs/Music: "Sheep Shearing," "Gdunko" (Norwegian folk song), Grieg's Symphonic Dance no. 4

Composer: Edvard Grieg

Australia

Songs/Music: "Australia's on the Wallaby," "Oma Rapeti," "Pukaea"

Musicians: Jay Coleman, Hinewehi Mohi

Antarctica

Songs/Music: "Antarctica," "Three Little Penguins"

Composer: Paul Winter

Grade 2 Answer Key

Resource Master 4-4
One, Two, or Three Beats

1.

2. Answers will vary. Make sure that students have followed the guidelines.

3.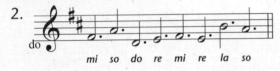

Resource Master 4-5
Do, Re, Mi, So, and *La*

2.

mi   so   do   re   mi   re   la   so

3.

do   re   mi   so   la   do

Resource Master 4-8
Mid-Unit Review

1. Answers will vary. Make sure students have a combination of notes and rests that equals 3 beats per measure.

2.

do   re   mi   so   la   so   do   re   do

3. c

Resource Master 4-10
Musical Questions and Answers

1. Q

2. A

3. Q

4. Answers will vary. Make sure that students have followed the guidelines.

Resource Master 4-11
American Indian Music

The drum and the rattle are blue.

Resource Master 5-4
Find the Rhythm

1. a or b

2. e

3. c or d

4. g or h

5. d or c

6. f

7. b or a

8. h or g

Resource Master 5-5
Pentatonic Scale

1. Alouette

do   re   mi   mi   re   do   re   mi   do   so (low)

2. The Farmer in the Dell

(low) so   do   do   do   do   do   re   m   mi   mi   mi   mi

3. Take Me Out to the Ball Game

(low) do (high) do   la   so   m   so   re (low) do (high) do   la   so   mi   so

Grade 2 Answer Key

Resource Master 5-8
Mid-Unit Review

1.

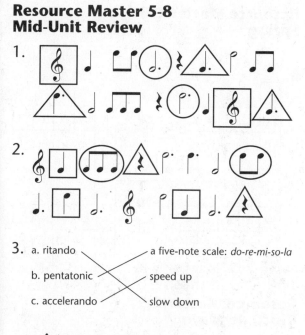

2.

3.

a. ritando   a five-note scale: *do-re-mi-so-la*

b. pentatonic   speed up

c. accelerando   slow down

4.

do   re   mi   so   la

Resource Master 5-10
Dixieland Instruments

Make sure that students have correctly identified the instruments.

Resource Master 6-4
Garden Rhythms

Answers will vary. Make sure that three-syllable words are paired with three eighth notes; two-syllable words are paired with a quarter and an eighth note; and one-syllable words are paired with a dotted quarter note.

Resource Master 6-6
Animal Rhythms

1. (African) Elephant

2. (Antarctica) Penguin

3. (Australian) Kangaroo

4. (Grizzly) Bear

5. (Bengal) Tiger

6. (Snowshoe) Hare

Resource Master 6-7
Pitching "Here Comes Sally"

Line 1: do, la, so, la, so, la, so, la

Line 2: do, la, so, la, mi, re, do

Resource Master 6-8
Mid-Unit Review

All of the Cs should be colored blue; the Es, yellow; the Gs, red; and the As, green.

Resource Master 6-9
Instrument Families

Strings: cello, viola, violin, double bass

Brass: trumpet, trombone, French horn, tuba

Woodwinds: clarinet, flute/piccolo, oboe, bassoon

Percussion: bass drum, snare drum, gong, timpani

Resource Master C-1
Fall Apple Harvest

1. a. PIE
   b. JUICE
   c. SAUCE
   d. BUTTER
   e. CIDER

Grade 2 Answer Key

Resource Master C-4
Hanukkah

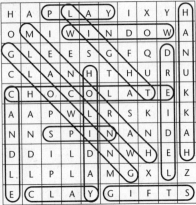

Resource Master C-5
Christmas

A man named JOSEPH and a woman named MARY went to BETHLEHEM to have a baby. Angels told the SHEPHERDS looking after their sheep to look for a baby in a MANGER sound asleep. Later came the WISE MEN, following a star, to bring the baby Jesus GIFTS from afar!

Resource Master C-8
Spring

4.

													1 R		
													A		
	2 F												I		
3 L	A	M	B							4 B	U	N	N	Y
O										A				
W				5 C	L	O	U	D	S				
E				H					K				
6 R	O	B	I	N				7 E	G	G	8 S	
S				C				T			U	
				K							N	

Resource Master C-9
Cinco de Mayo

1. d
2. c
3. e
4. a
5. b